AROUND THE NEXT CORNER

A GUIDE TO MAPPING YOUR FUTURE

About the author

Writer, lecturer and broadcaster Jillie Collings was born and educated in Australia where she read English and History. With her first novel in her luggage, she left Australia for London in the mid-sixties to begin a completely new career as an investigatory journalist, specialising in health, psychology and the paranormal.

There she undertook further studies in Astrology, Palmistry and Graphology and subsequently wrote the Astrology column for *Woman* magazine for ten years. She has recently completed a series in *The Guardian* on modern health concepts ('Life Forces') which is to become the subject of her next book.

Around the Next Corner

A Guide to Mapping your Future

Jillie Collings

NEW ENGLISH LIBRARY
Hodder and Stoughton

Copyright © Jillie Collings 1990

First published in Great Britain in 1990 by New English Library hardbacks

New English Library paperback edition 1991

British Library C.I.P.

Collings, Jillie
  Around the next corner.
  1. Prophecy
  I. Title
  133.3
  ISBN 0-450-54292-0

Printed and bound in Great Britain for Hodder and Stoughton Paperbacks, a division of Hodder and Stoughton Ltd., Mill Road, Dunton Green, Sevenoaks, Kent TN13 2YA (Editorial Office: 47 Bedford Square, London WC1B 3DP) by Clays Ltd., St Ives plc.

Change is the only constant

Contents

Part Three

ACKNOWLEDGMENTS

Many people have shown interest in this book as I have been writing it. Their support in helping me to pin down the unpinnable world of those who try to map our future for us has been considerable. In particular I am grateful to those experts who willingly gave me interviews, thus allowing me to avail myself of their considerable experience, namely (in alphabetical order) palmist/author, Mir Bashir; geomancer/psychic, David Bingham; astrologer/author, Zipporah Dobyns; psychic/author, Peter Lee; philosopher/psychiatrist/author, Raymond Moody; graphologist/author, Renna Nezos; psychic/medium, Owen Potts; Tarot-card reader/writer, John Christopher Travers; psychic/medium, David Young.

Others helped me with suggestions over the telephone or wrote giving me copious help with addresses for the Directory in Part 3, and I would like to proffer special thanks in this respect (again in alphabetical order) to Madge Copeland of Victoria, Australia; Mette Forum of Copenhagen; Harry Gullefer, Secretary of the Society for the Study of Physiological Patterns, U.K.; Charles Harvey, President of the U.K. Astrological Association; Dr Alfred Hug, President of Astrolabe Computer Programmes in Lausanne, Switzerland; Herbert Larsen, Astrologer (Hamburg); Neil Michelson, President of Astro Computing Services in San Diego, California; So Mak (for his far-flung contacts gathered while travelling for the Hong Kong Tourist Association in his capacity as a fortune-teller); Friedrich Pestalozzi, Spiritualist and President of Bio-strath AG (who has helped me so many times with so many projects); David Shaw, Secretary of the British Institute of Graphologists, and Ray Webb, Editor/Publisher of the Australian magazine *Astrological Monthly Review* (for the flow of information and feedback and for offering the services of his magazine as a clearing house for Australian enquiries) ... to these in particular and to many others in general.

I would also like to express thanks to my agent Jane Judd, whose help and support was given from the moment she first read the synopsis and well before she ever set up her literary agency; to Stanley Gander, whose patience in teaching me word-processing was (and still is) monumental; to my husband Ben for reading the manuscript and making many useful suggestions; to my friend Biata Bishop for always having her contacts book at the ready, and last but never least, to my friend and counsellor Barbara Somers, who has helped me around so many corners that I have lost count of them.

I also wish to express my grateful acknowledgments to the following authors and periodicals whose work has been of invaluable help: Colin Wilson for *The Occult* by permission of Hodder & Stoughton Ltd, Raymond Moody for *The Light Beyond*, Cherry Gilchrist for *Divination*; Peter Lee for *The Spirit Calls*; Sasha Fenton for *The Fortune-teller's Workbook*; Ruth Montgomery for *The Phenomenal Jeanne Dixon*; *Time Magazine*; and the *Journal of the American Medical Association*.

FOREWORD

There are many ways of predicting the future, and many books have been written trying to explain those ways to the lay public. They are a constant fascination, as the many titles devoted to them bear witness. However they do not take into account just how few people have either the time or the aptitude to learn a technique well enough by which to predict the future. So the reason for purchasing such a book is often defeated before one has even started, despite the overwhelming interest in discovering techniques which are able to afford one a glimpse of the pattern of one's life – especially of the future.

Colin Wilson, in his definitive book *The Occult*, has presented evidence from a variety of sources which indicate that only 5 per cent of the population have developed the ability to utilise techniques such as these drawing on what he calls "Faculty X", which embraces what others such as myself might call sixth sense or extra-sensory perception (ESP).*

Although he (in my view, rightly) believes that these gifts are innate in us all and as such it must be assumed that any latent ability can be developed, it is equally my belief that only years of exhaustive study and mental training will substitute for a deficit of Faculty X, which will not help beginners who will want to run before they walk, and who will need as large a share of Faculty X as they can muster if they are to profit from their DIY purchase.

Hence this book is not written for the 5 per cent who have always

---

* Faculty X, as Wilson describes it, comprises a constellation of special talents and abilities besides those we may think of as extra-sensory, and I refer those who wish to understand the wider concept to Wilson's books, particularly *The Occult*. In the course of this book only those aspects of Faculty X will be examined which have particular reference to abilities to transcend time, that is, to "know" the past, present and future as one.

had an innate psychic gift which needs only to be honed by picking up a technique: it is written for all the other 95 per cent who are longing to know about their future, but simply do not know where to look, who to ask, which of the techniques to choose, or what to make of the information they are told when they *do* choose ... factors which are critical to the result.

This book is a guide to the guides. It is designed to help you understand the way in which these techniques work and how to get the most out of what can be very nebulous information gained from them. It tells you how to consult the experts, how to discern the genuine from the ingenious. And how, having consulted them, to decipher and deploy the information you have received, so that you may progress in life not from hindsight, but with foresight.

Information from these sources can be considered as a kind of roadmap to the future. It does not tell us which route to take, but it does provide us with a view of the options. However, for a roadmap to be of any use, its keys and references have to be decoded and the same is true of information about the future, especially in respect to timing of events. Roadmaps are familiar objects to us now, easily decoded, but they must have looked more like mazes than maps the first time we ever peered at them over our parents' shoulders. And so it may seem with information about the future, which is often couched in ambiguous phrases which can even appear to be trivial. It is after all occult* or hidden knowledge which is being dispensed and as such needs special disciplines, most of them quite simple, in order to take advantage of what it has to say.

That is the purpose of this book – to unveil the mysteries of the prediction business, to examine techniques of foretelling from the seers to the piers and to explore how to go about finding experts who will do your future the justice it deserves.

---

* A common misconception exists that the word *occult* means *sinister*: it simply means *that which is hidden from general view*.

THE STORY BEHIND

AROUND THE NEXT CORNER

I was introduced to the prediction business in 1965 when I arrived in England from my native Australia with a sentence of death over my head. Doctors in Australia had said that they believed me to be suffering from leukaemia. However, their tests were inconclusive and since they were not able to be repeated before I was due to embark for England, they instructed colleagues in London to repeat the tests on my arrival.

During the five-week sea voyage, I died a thousand times. My hair went white. I shook uncontrollably and could not play deck sports (so loved on a previous voyage) because of the stiffness in my limbs – caused, I now realise, by tension.

Upon my arrival in London the lengthy business of repeating the tests began, and while I waited in that strange and overwhelmingly alien city where I knew no one and could seek solace from nobody, I stumbled one day upon a house with an unusual nameplate at its door. It announced the presence of a palmist. On the spur of the moment I made an appointment – my first ever with a so-called fortune-teller. What did I have to lose?

The palmist I consulted was first-class, as I later discovered, and he told me that I would not die prematurely as I feared, but would live a full life-span. I did not altogether believe him at the time: the doctors' predictions had burned themselves too deeply into my brain. Furthermore, their word carried the mighty weight of the medical profession behind it.

Yet the palmist told me so many other things that were accurate, especially about my past (including the year of my father's death) that I had to pay attention to him. Furthermore, as he conducted the reading I observed that the techniques he was using were more scientific than empirical. He took handprints: he measured lines and skin-ridge patterns with precise little geometrical instruments:

he even marked off several lines on my hand with a millimetre scale.

Before the session was over, I found myself asking him where I could learn this fascinating study. I had almost forgotten about my sentence of death, so exhilarated was I about a prospect I had never before imagined: that the outlines of one's destiny could be mapped and therefore conceivably even influenced for the better!

Not daunted by the palmist's laconic reply to my question – that if I wanted to learn palmistry I would have to go and sit on the banks of the Brahmaputra river in India (or was it the Ganges?) and wait for a Master to appear, I discovered that there were classes much closer to home – in London to be precise. I enrolled for a beginner's course and began working immediately on all available guinea pigs – the hands of my family and new-found friends.

I soon realised that the basic tenets of palmistry were irrefutable, based as they were on the fundamental truth that no two sets of fingerprints – or indeed handprints – in the world were alike and as such they needs must represent a unique pattern of the individual under study: a physiological pattern characteristic of that one person and none other. The problem, as I saw it, was in de-coding the pattern accurately, for I quickly discovered that subjects such as palmistry had inevitably suffered from not being taught and researched in universities or recognised schools of learning for what amounted (in the West) to centuries. Thus the first-class minds normally associated with advanced education had not applied themselves to palmistry: instead it had been handed down, often verbally, through generation upon generation of fortune-tellers. Or worse, it had attracted the attention of those who sought to gain power over others by setting themselves up as seers and prophets. It was to a handful of pioneers (some of them doctors) who had looked at palmistry with enlightened eyes that we owed the few worth-while text books and research programmes that had been preserved for us to study.

Other sobering implications of delving into one's future soon presented themselves to me: while examining my son's hand I discovered a line which the text books clearly represented as an indication of the loss of a close family member.

Immediately all my old fears were re-constellated. Was I still to die, just as I had discovered a whole world of exciting prospects to live for? The lines crossed my son's life-line at the age of seven. (He was then four.) Did I have but three years to live?

I took the prints to the palmist I had originally consulted, who told me that I was making the same mistake that all beginners make – interpreting to the extreme. "A loss does not necessarily mean a death," he pointed out. "Go back home and think about it."

I did, and realised that he had already predicted from my own hand the very event which I had seen in my son's. He had told me on our first meeting to expect "a disappointment in love in about three years' time" – something I would not be able to influence or change because it was not largely of my own making.

In exactly that period of time my husband left me to go to America. It was something he had secretly planned for years, and both my son's hand and my own had somehow recognised this impending loss. It was as if we had known it "in our hearts". My teachers had taught me (and I had seen for myself) that event lines on the hand changed, sometimes quite quickly, as we made decisions which influenced the course of our lives. But sometimes (or so it seemed to them) we were the victims rather than the sculptors of our destiny. This was when events happened "out of the blue" that we did nót wish or want. Yet at other times we seemed to be able favourably to manipulate our fates to our own advantage! Suddenly I saw that they were not two separate conditions, they were interlinked: that it was only when the weight of what others were planning for us was greater than what we had planned for ourselves that fate seemed to step in and put us on a course which we did not altogether like or anticipate. Surely then, the stronger and more defined we were in our plans for the future, the less likely this was to happen.

Once I had argued myself through to this conclusion I realised that there was a very good case to be presented for delving into our future prospects. If we are the architects of our future (and I believe we are) then the more we know about ourselves, our abilities, what we want out of life and our potential to get it, the better. And if this involves consulting experts who can tell us more about our future potential, then let us do so – not to accept what they predict or pronounce as written on tablets of stone, but in order to begin to shape and sculpt that stone.

In time I was to investigate many methods for foretelling the future and eventually I became qualified in the three doctrines I felt most at home with: astrology, palmistry and graphology. Additionally, and in the course of my work as a journalist and feature-writer, I was to delve still more deeply into the practices and practitioners of the fortune-telling arts. I uncovered many talented people but regrettably I also uncovered far too many frauds – people who had a gift but were not prepared to develop it, people who had a gift which came and went depending on daily events, and worst of all, people who had a gift and used it to wield power over those whose fortunes they told, either through extracting extortionate fees or by frightening them into return visits and thereby controlling their lives. I am sure this is why many intelligent and otherwise open-minded people are so against fortune-telling and delving into the future: they have seen the harm which can be done.

Yet – to create an analogy – modern drugs used by the medical profession can also do harm, but they are not discarded holus-bolus because of their unpleasant and even dangerous side-effects. Rather they are used with restraint. Surely the same sort of attitude could and should be applied to the utility of fortune-telling.

However if one looks at this opposition, arising as it often does from highly influential groups within society such as scientists and men of religion, an interesting pattern emerges. For the nature of the opposition suggests not so much reasoned doubt on their part as a pathological fear, coupled with a desire to reject without fair test or trial anything which smacks of fortune-telling or prognostication of the future. There is a complete absence of open-mindedness.

In delving into the wispy strands of the history of fortune-telling, an indication of the origin of such deep-seated and passionate and illogical suspicions may be found. Not long ago psychics, clairvoyants, and anyone who professed to tell fortunes, were persecuted as witches and burned at the stake. As many as 300,000 of society's most gifted women intuitives were estimated to have lost their lives in this way. This must have engendered in those remaining an almighty fear of being seen in the company of anyone reputed to have these "special gifts" and it is possible that this fear remains stored in the unconscious racial memory today. Or alternatively it could simply be that the preponderance of rationally-oriented minds that remained to breed, have influenced the structure and composition of Western society for many generations, upsetting the balance of the 5 per cent who possess extraordinary gifts of consciousness. No one could deny that we currently belong to an age dominated by reason, if not dogma, a world in which intuition is only just beginning to resurface as a worthy faculty.

Yet with modern, often scientific research enlightening us day by day about the intangibility of some of the factors which influence our lives and the forces within us, it is surely timely to discard prejudices which were thrust upon us by previous generations who were not able to know what we know now. Hopefully we will come full-circle, from persecuting fortune-tellers to encouraging, researching and constructively invigilating them and most of all incorporating them and the very real gifts they have to offer into our modern society.

It is more than twenty years since I first stumbled into my initial consultation with a fortune-teller – although I am sure that the venerable Mir Bashir, whom I consulted, would not thank me for calling him a fortune-teller, which is why I have coined a new word in this book for this group of talented people – *foretellers*.

Much that I have learned over that twenty years has been incorporated into this book, in the hope that others may not have to stumble quite so blindly to discover, and learn to build on, their exciting potentials for the future.

PART ONE

1
INTRODUCTION
Common Dilemmas In Consulting Foretellers

Most people want to know what is around the next corner – provided
it is good. But behind that proviso lies a very real fear – fear of the
future, of what it might hold, that it might not be good at all. It is
that very fear which keeps many people away from foretellers'
doors. It keeps them away, that is, until the very moment when they
are at their most vulnerable: when they have reached a crossroads
in life and have to make a vital decision. Then in a fit of desperation,
wanting only to be relieved of the burden of taking a step which
may well change the course of their lives, they bear the tender
foetus of their unborn future to what is frequently an ill-considered
source of information.

People, normally sensible people, who would not dream of
selecting their doctor, lawyer or other professional consultant in
such a devil-may-care manner, will freely admit that they wandered
into the first foreteller they saw (or who would see them) when they
were confronted with that numinous and powerful instinct which
signifies an impending change in life.

To say that such an act is potentially foolhardy is to say the least,
but it is an understandable error which is made every day because
there is not enough information available about how to make such
an informed choice. Few realise that just as there are specialists in
professions like medicine and the law, equally there are specialists
in the prediction business.

Some techniques are better suited to certain lines of enquiry
than others. For example, if there has been a recent death in the
family and you wish to know where the reputedly missing last will
is hidden, it is no good going to an astrologer or a palmist: you
would need to go to a medium – a person who is equipped to
mediate between this world and the next, and hope that your

3

presence there will inspire your dead relative to convey through the medium where the missing will is hidden!

Thus it is that all techniques used by foretellers are in fact horses for courses. Some techniques employ and can only be plied by those who have a highly developed extra-sensory or sixth sense (now more commonly known as extra-sensory perception or ESP for short). Techniques such as clairvoyance, crystal-gazing, psychometry (to name three), invariably incorporate a psychic or intuitive faculty. Others, such as graphology (which has already gained professional status and is being taught in some universities), can be learned as any science can be learned. Graphology is well suited to the assessment of character and potential and thus is much employed by head-hunters and those engaged in personnel selection.

In fact all techniques employed by foretellers can and should be learned, although it would be equally true to say that only some can learn them. But another common and most dangerous mistake made by the general public is to believe that none of the techniques can be learned and as such the seeking or demanding of proof of any kind of qualification or training from the people they plan to consult is irrelevant.

Whilst there is little doubt that a true seer is born and not made, it surely follows that as with all inherited gifts such as for musical ability or for painting, training is an essential part of the development of that talent and will invariably result in a refinement of the techniques and an improvement in the performance. The training of seers and prophets has long been a tradition in the East, where such gifts have been respected throughout history and have not suffered the serious drawbacks of persecution and ridicule that have occurred in the West.

Training has one other vital benefit in this area apart from improvement in proficiency, in that it usually incorporates instruction in a method or code of practice. Students are encouraged to understand the ramifications of what they are telling their clients and the likely after-effects. Most doctrines taught in this way have formulated a code of ethics (much like the Hippocratic oath) to which student graduates are expected to adhere, and many incorporate counselling techniques.

If all this seems irrelevant to the simple expedient of having your fortune told, it is far from so. It is a well-known fact that most people will forget any dire warnings their doctor may offer (such as what will happen if they do not give up drinking to excess or smoking) almost as soon as they vacate the doctor's surgery. But a prognostication of death or disaster from a foreteller will produce in the same person a trauma which is never forgotten and is often the cause of prolonged mental anguish.

There is another reason why evidence of some kind of training, qualification or experience should be insisted upon and that is because it will inevitably lead to a general improvement in the quality and standard of information made available in this way. Admittedly, were this condition ever to become law (as well might happen), it could lead initially to the exclusion of some gifted amateurs, but that is a small price to pay for invigilating and quality-controlling a vocation which has always attracted more than its fair share of charlatans.*

It is also becoming increasingly obvious to leading experts in this field that some kind of counselling training should be an essential part of any teaching programme formulated for those who look into future trends. It has long been observed that some otherwise talented people who work in this area either do not know or do not care about the effect they have on those who consult them. Clients frequently complain that they are rushed out into the street after being told of a major disruption in their lives before they have even caught their breath! Some have then had to drive home through busy traffic in what is virtually a state of shock – and they are usually unaccompanied because they have not told anybody where they are going! This is not to suggest that every visit to a foreteller results in the uncovering of traumatic material, but it can raise deep emotional issues which have hitherto been repressed and it can convey news that puts one off-balance. It is for this reason that the directory section of this book includes counselling organisations who are used to dealing with this sort of contingency.

Other points to be covered in the text (which may seem irrelevant

* See overview of this issue in Chapter 15, "*Helping yourself to your future*".

5

but which are in fact highly relevant) concern the vital issues of selecting a suitable consultant and also the provision of guidelines to the manner in which the consultation should be conducted. This is because the nature of the information that can be derived from these sources is so volatile and so easily affected by personalities, both on this side and on the other, that seemingly unimportant details can have great bearing on the results obtained. Thus the whole process of the reading or sitting, as it is often called, has been gone into thoroughly.

For those who may be interested in learning one of the foretelling techniques for themselves (for this subject is a constant fascination) there is a guide to the courses available (in Part 3) and also a book-list for each doctrine (at the end of each chapter in Part 2). The books mentioned in the bibliography are diverse in nature, comprising introductory and popular titles, as well as titles which indicate what research and investigation has revealed about each field; yet other works of reference may be helpful in the studying at least of the more established techniques, such as astrology, palmistry and graphology.

Studying of techniques which rely more on the psychic faculty is usually done in groups and some of these have been listed in Part 3 – but of more value, most probably, is the little guide there called *How to Look*. Because of the very nature of these studies in that they are occult, special techniques are sometimes needed to uncover sources of knowledge.

For the majority of readers, who will be interested in consulting experts for themselves rather than learning techniques, there is a directory (in Part 3) not of personalities but of professional groups whose job it is to direct enquirers to relevant experts in their area. But it should be remembered that this work is frequently performed by gifted individuals who tend to shun professional conglomerates and it may take both time, and a few failures, to find the expert most suited to the needs of each individual.

If all this seems to be advocating a rather laborious and labyrinthine approach to what has hitherto been regarded more as a fair-ground diversion, it is because my experience as a consultant has shown that clients do not come in with light-hearted questions.

They come in with momentous questions, to do with their most intimate relationships, their careers and their health. And it would seem that they are not questions which they feel comfortable about referring to more traditional lines of assistance, such as general practitioners, ministers of religion or social workers. The reasons given for preferring the anonymity of foretellers are many and varied, but they include not wanting to have a record made of their predicament in medical or official files, not wanting to be morally judged, or not wanting to make a decision in a matter until they have explored every avenue, including what might lie in the future!

If that is the case, then there is a very real place in society for the very real talents that foretelling has to offer. The ensuing chapters are an attempt to help would-be explorers to achieve the best of all possible results.

2
BEFORE TAKING THE PLUNGE
Guide to the Correct Choice

Let us suppose a situation has arisen in your life which presents a challenge. You have to respond but you are not sure what your response should be. You only know that it is important – that ideally you would like to explore pathways and possibilities open to you before taking any action.

What you would really like to know is what is likely to happen in the future. There is not much point changing horses in midstream, for example, if the relieving horse does not feel like swimming! You would dearly love to know what is around the next corner.

You decide to consult a foreteller. How do you go about it? Do you telephone a friend or two and ask whom they consulted? Do you go to your local newsagent and buy a publication which contains pages of advertisements relevant to this field? Or do you simply wander down to your local market and wait outside the fortune-teller's stall?

Hopefully you will do none of these things until you have thoroughly examined your motives, not because your motives are important in themselves, but because, once classified, they will point you in the direction of the appropriate expert.

But first you will need to ask yourself one very important question and that is: how long are you able to wait for your consultation – how urgent is the situation? Does it require a response from you tomorrow, or next week?

Obviously, the more time you have, the better the choices you can make. Many consultants have long waiting lists, though if your case is really urgent, they will very often try to fit you in. However, a consultant who is fitting you in is under pressure, and in this volatile field that can mean poorer results or less consultation time.

8

So the earlier you can decide to consult someone about an up-and-coming problem, the better. Do not leave it until the problem is right on your doorstep, because it may result in a second-rate consultant, or a second-rate consultation.

Motives

Your motives and the type of information you are seeking will have direct bearing on what category of foreteller you decide to see. As intimated in Chapter 1, not all foretellers work in the same way and their results can be worlds apart – which may explain why so many people experience failures and disappointments in this area.

So your first deliberation should be to consider the situation which has arisen in your life and to ask yourself what sort of information will help you most in making a decision. For example: is yours a specific, isolated question, such as whether to accept an invitation to go on holiday with a colleague at work? (In which case all you would need to know is whether you and your colleague were compatible and whether the proposed destination was mutually acceptable.) Or do you suspect that your colleague's invitation has wider, more general implications which may lead to an offer which could change the course of your life?

Therefore you must decide: what sort of information is going to have the most value to me in making my decision? Astrologers, for example, are very good at working on general patterns and trends in your life, and although they can and do answer specific questions about a love object, a health consultation, a career meeting, etc, they prefer to deal with general guidelines, to lay down the roadmap of the period ahead but not to describe the route or who you may meet en route.

Clairvoyants, on the other hand, love working with intimate detail and like nothing better than to be asked a specific question. They can vividly describe who you may meet en route but may not necessarily know what page of the roadmap you are on. Could be this year's, next year's ... Sometimes they are accurate with timing, sometimes it does not seem to have relevance.

If your question is important, it is a good plan to try one line of enquiry first, then another. Funnily enough, this rarely occurs to people seeking this sort of advice: it is as if their first failure is proof of the pudding that the prediction system does not work. (The same people will move mountains to try to find a decent dentist or a reliable butcher.)

However, in all fairness it should be noted here that information about the future is not always forthcoming when we want it. Simply, "the matter is not ready for judging" – as the great Madeline Montalban, a leading occultist of our times, used to say. This was not a remark of convenience after a failed reading, but simply a comment upon the complexities of our inter-relationships, the outcomes of which depend upon each other's free-will. Enough pieces have to be entered into the jig-saw before a picture begins to form. (Montalban always used to advise the querent to wait for a few months, then try again.)

Categorising Your Motive

In order to find your most appropriate source of information it is important to identify your motive with one of the headings you will find at the end of this chapter, that is, under considerations of love, money, career, health, special situation, interest in general trends, etc.

Once you have done this (most people have two or three lines of enquiry) you can then begin to write the questions which you would like to have answered under each heading. Try to put the categories and their various questions in order of importance and try to keep the list as compact as you can. Many consultants prefer you to limit the number of questions you ask because too many can confuse the major points of issue. (Which, by the way, they may perceive to be different from your list of priorities!)

Refining Your Choice

Once you have selected the mode of the sitting or reading by identifying the main category of your desired information, you can begin to look for a specific expert. There is a directory in Part 3 of this book with names and addresses of organisations who will recommend an expert in your area. However it is wise to be prepared to travel if you are at all unsure of the local product when the contact is made. To that effect it is advisable to ask the organisation to suggest several consultants with the facility in answering your line of enquiry.

If you cannot wait for information of this kind to arrive, you can buy one of the publications listed in the directory which carry advertisements of appropriate experts. However, you must then be prepared for the hit-and-miss results that you may encounter, and if the outcome proves unsatisfactory you will need to try again.

Considerations of Time

Time of Birth. If you are intending to seek an astrological reading it is essential to ascertain your correct time of birth. Since an error of four minutes *can* lead to an astrologer making an error of up to a year in some of your predictions for the future, you are advised to make every effort to see that this piece of information is as accurate as you can get it. Birth times have always been recorded on birth certificates by some countries (e.g. Scotland and France) but have only been recorded by others (e.g. England) in the last few decades. However, it is advisable to write to the hospital where you were born as some hospitals have always kept their own private records. It should also be noted that officially-recorded birth certificate times may have been rounded off to the nearest quarter of an hour by busy hospital staff so having a family member at hand at every birth, armed with a stop-watch to record the first breath drawn of the new-born, is not such a foolish practice. Place of birth will also be required as this too is used in the calculations in order to establish the sidereal (or star-time) of your birth.

If you were not born in a hospital, it always helps to question older relatives closely, as memories may conflict. Mother may remember that it was breakfast time, which can be vague, but father may remember that he was just about to leave to catch his customary train, and that will narrow down the inaccuracy.

Timing

Timing of anticipated events given in readings is one of the most difficult aspects of predictive work. This is because, as has already been mentioned, much of the information is passed to the consultant from a source in which time does not exist: what is euphemistically called "the other side". And although "the other side" can be spot-on with timing, they can also be hideously astray! It is as if the timing of some events in our lives is not as critical as it is of others. Either that, or, at the time of the reading, it is not ready to be judged correctly.

Possibly the best guide for the timing of events is astrology since it is a study based on the timing of the movements of the planets which themselves reflect events in our lives. The planets are simply cosmic clocks and as such events in the future can often be accurately assessed from them. However, it is not as simple as it seems, because some planets form and re-form the same aspect several times over what may be as long as a two-year period. So what is the poor astrologer to do – which of the several formations is going to lead to the event he *knows* will happen? Sometimes other planets will give the clue, sometimes not. So querents need to be reasonably philosophical about timing, and not regard what has been said as having been pronounced by the astrological equivalent of Big Ben. Some of the most accurate assessments of time have been given to me by palmist Mir Bashir. He has usually been able to predict the year in which an event would happen, but even Bashir has been wrong on one or two occasions. Astrologers can sometimes be even more accurate than just to within a given year: author/astrologer Grant Lewi was said to have assessed his exact day of death, and to have taken out insurance accordingly!

Personal Preferences

The guide at the end of this chapter is meant to be just that – a general guide. There can be no set rules when seeking information about your future and if you find a consultant who genuinely suits you and seems to be able to give you pertinent advice, but is not specifically recommended in the guide for your type of enquiry, do not necessarily consider you may do better elsewhere. There are clairvoyants who are wonderful with timing (despite what has been written about them here), there are fairground fortune-tellers who are as good as, or better, than the well-known seers of their day. There simply are no set rules, only guidelines. But what you may find is that some experts seem to be more "on your wavelength" than others. But do not try to see the same person, however good, more than once a year. They can become genuinely confused between what they learn about you during a sitting and what they are learning about you through other means.

Recommendations

This is possibly the best way to find an expert. Most of the good, established people working in these fields do not even advertise. They are often booked up months in advance, so it is advisable, if you find them helpful, to make an appointment for a regular sitting every year. Then, if you find you do not need it you can always cancel – hopefully well before the appointed day!

Consultation Patterns

The previous point raises the vexed issue of regularly consulting experts about your future, which critics believe encourages living in the future rather than the reality of today. Basically I think it is a good thing to have regular top-ups with foretellers, since it keeps you in touch with your options. All too often in life we miss our best chances by not being prepared for them. Most of us sense long before an event occurs that it is "in the offing", but we do not like to really think about it too carefully in case we are "tempting providence". So when the offer does eventuate, usually quite quickly, we have not prepared the key negotiating points. As a result we lose that liquid moment when conditions can be imposed and deals can be struck. The other side has taken advantage of the element of surprise, leaving us, the acceders, on the other end of the initiative. This can happen in any area of life, from proposals of marriage, when the chance to lay down certain vital stipulations (such as preferred areas in which to live) can be lost, to multi-million-pound business deals where one vital point can be over-looked in the surprise of the moment. We may consider going back for another bite of the negotiating cherry, but we know in our hearts that the time for striking bargains is passed. So it is provident to keep well in touch with future options, in that they allow you to prepare, not for certainties, but for marked possibilities.

Considerations of Cost

It is difficult to put a price on consultations when their length can vary from ten minutes or so to two and a half hours – especially when ten minutes of vital information can technically be of more value than two and a half hours of waffle. However, time *is* money and some of these techniques, such as astrology, require the expert to spend several hours of intensive preparation before the actual reading. So expect to pay a top consultant at the rate you would pay a medical specialist, keeping in mind that the consultation time given by a medical specialist is rarely more than half an hour.

Always establish the fee before you go and a method of payment which will be acceptable.

Ramifications

Do you *really* want to know what is around the next corner for you – regardless of whether it is good or bad? Because if you are not prepared to live with the worst that you can be told as well as the best, you should not try to find out at all. Not that you should accept the worst in a fatalistic way – the whole purpose of going to a foreteller is to make the best of your options: to find out about your future in time to change it. Even dire prognostications can be averted, although it has been observed that in some of life's up and coming issues we do seem to have less option to influence their outcome than in others. Nevertheless we must always try.

There will be times when a destructive foreteller may forecast alarming things. If this happens it is always wise to check with another expert, or to wait a few months, until whatever "black cloud" around you has dispersed. Depression and illness, fatigue and other emotions, both of the consultant and of the querent, can affect results. Tarot-card readers in particular know it is unwise to read the cards when they are upset or tired; yet how can they cancel a day's appointments when people may have been waiting several weeks to see them? It takes a very strong conviction to do such a thing.

So do not be too thrown by bad news, but on the other hand do be prepared to face it if you are going to consult foretellers. It is a fact of life that we rarely consult foretellers when things are going well, so inevitably there is likely to be some problem around us at the time of the sitting.

Guide to Choosing Your Consultant

Most experts would agree that there are four main reasons why people consult them, namely considerations of love, finance, family, or proposed (or feared) changes in life conditions. However, the means by which they seek their information varies greatly (some may bring an object belonging to a key person in their dilemma, some may bring a scrap of handwriting, others may expect the foreteller to be the means between the querent and the information desired). Whatever the technique, it is often the means by which the information is sought that governs the method chosen. For example, there is little point in consulting an astrologer if you do not have an accurate birth time, just as there is little point in going to see a Tarot-card reader if you do not really believe in the cards – your attitude will prejudice the outcome.

The following guide is intended to give you as comprehensive a list of choices as possible. However, there is one other important factor to bear in mind and that is that there are basically two types of readings available:

1. Readings which are based on a knowledge of one of the doctrines, for example, astrology, palmistry, graphology, that is, where a body of knowledge has been learned by the consultant and most likely a diploma attained.

2. Readings which are based on ESP (psychic gift, intuition, trans, trance or channelling ability) which virtually includes all other forms of foretelling, most practitioners of which are usually referred to as psychics or clairvoyants.

Such people may well have trained exhaustively to arrive at their level of skill, but because of the extremely individualistic way in which such gifts are manifested, they usually train singly or in small groups and do not receive diplomas – although some do pass proficiency tests.

If you prefer to think that your consultation has been structured by some background or body of knowledge, then it is obvious that you would feel more at home with one of the techniques incorporating a doctrine.

If you are one of those who like to make up their minds to see somebody on the spur of the moment, then you would probably be better suited (and more quickly served) by choosing someone in the second category.

Guide to Choosing an Expert

Chosen Category

General Trends (period of a few weeks up to 6 months)	Tarot
General Trends (12 months, 2 or 3 special areas of interest)	Astrology
General Trends (2–5 years) with or without cross-checked results	Astrology, Palmistry
Vocational and Career Skills	Astrology, Graphology
Vocational/Employment/Career Plans & Moves	Astrology
Money Problems & Investments	Astrology, Tarot, Psychics
Proposed Moves of Location	Astrocartography, Tarot, Crystal Gazing
Buying & Selling of Homes, Business & Property	Astrology, Tarot, Clairvoyance

Health (general trends)	Palmistry, Psychics, esp. Medical Clairvoyance
Health (specific question or issue – such as pregnancy or not)	Psychics
Romance (what lies ahead)	Psychics, Palmistry
Romance (compatibility)	Graphology, Astrology (synastry)
Romance (love problems)	Psychic/Astrologer with counselling ability
Family Matters & Issues	Psychics, Astrology, Tarot
Children (for guidance from birth, with birth-time)	Astrology
Children (without natal chart)	Classify reason and look there
Partnership & Marital Problems	Astrologer/Psychic with wide counselling experience (preferably a diploma)
Partnership Problems (other designations)	Astrology, Psychics
Deep, Searing Problems	Astrological, Transpersonal or Psychic counsellors
Unexpected Development/Special Situation	Horary Astrology, Psychics
Robberies and Missing Objects	Clairvoyance, Horary Astrology
Finding out about Someone with Handwriting Sample	Psychics, Graphology
Contacting a Person who has Died	Trans-channeller (medium)
Immediate (DIY) Answer to Pressing Problem	I Ching
Light-hearted look into the Future (but beware!)	Fairground/Market fortune-teller

3
PREPARATION
Forewarning and Forearming

The next three chapters contain advice about the actual process of having a consultation with an expert in the foretelling field, that is *preparation, consultation* and *aftermath*. These chapters discuss the three vital stages in the acquisition, distillation and digestion of any information you may obtain about your future and although much of this discourse may seem more like plain common sense than revelations about the occult, it is wise to skim through it in order to avoid making unnecessary mistakes.

In my early days as an investigatory journalist exploring the psychic world, I wasted valuable information about my own future (as well as valuable time belonging to my editors) simply by not understanding the process needed for extracting this special kind of information. However, for the impatient (and for later quick reference) I have summarised the salient points at the end of each chapter.

Contacting Your Chosen Consultant

The process of making the appointment with the consultant you have tentatively chosen will immediately tell you a variety of things. We are generally taught to suppress our first impressions and to let reason dominate, but this is one time when your intuition should be switched on as you settle the following issues:

1. Date, time, length and cost of appointment.

2. Whether you can tape the session and if so do you need to bring your own recording equipment or just a tape?

3. Is there anything else you are required to bring such as an object for psychometry, a photograph, or other?

4. Last but not least (assuming you like the way your conversation

has gone), establish thorough directions and an estimated length of time of your journey.

Some of these points may seem obvious, but my experience over the years from both sides of the consultation table has convinced me that even the most down-to-earth people get into a state akin to visiting the dentist when they make appointments to see foretellers. Part of them does not want to obey the part that has made the appointment and this sort of internal war often manifests in silly little ways, like getting the address wrong, forgetting to bring a tape, or lateness – all of which are deleterious to the end result.

One other possibility needs exploration: what happens if you do not like the sound of the person you have chosen? Before changing your mind (and please tell your first choice if you do) it is as well to bear in mind that people who work in this field *are* out-of-the-ordinary. Many psychics I have contacted sounded as if they were at the end of a very long distance call when in fact they were in the same area. There is a remoteness about some foretellers which should not be misconstrued as diffidence or even abruptness. So unless you feel distinctly uncomfortable or sense that your overtures are unwelcome – possibly due to overwork – think twice before you change your choice.

Some consultants still require requests in writing. They are usually astrologers, who hope that by requiring you to write down the date, time and place of your birth you are less likely to get it wrong. Some of the remaining few are hopeful that if you commit your intention to paper, you will be more likely to turn up. Many astrologers will ask you to send all or part of the fee in advance: this is because much of the work has to be done in advance and is quite legitimate in their case, *but rarely in other cases.* (Graphology by post is another legitimate exception.)

A few foretellers – very few these days – prefer only to do written work and will not see clients at all. Certainly this is true of consultant graphologists who do not wish to be confused between what they see on the page and what they see before them! In my capacity as a graphologist I prefer to work by mail, although I will often look at the handwriting within the structure of a general consultation, for cross-checking and other purposes.

Incredible as it may seem, some psychics can actually work at a distance from their subject, so do not necessarily be put off by a reader who will not see you. Edgar Cayce, the famous American prophet, always worked this way, and the accuracy of his readings was substantiated a countless number of times by the thousands who had them.

Readers who are familiar with radionics (which is a form of health dowsing) will not find this remote concept so strange. It is as if the psychic picks up a radio signal on your very own frequency. New research is just beginning to indicate how this process may work – that each of us has an electromagnetic field around us which is unique and which does give out a weak signal which a "sensitive" such as a person with ESP can pick up. So if you live a long way from the person you really want to consult, investigate the possibility of sending them an object which has long been in your possession, or a photograph. I recently had a superb health reading from America by just those means.

For the scientific die-hards, who simply will not entertain the concept of remote readings, I remind them that it was not so very long ago (1876 to be precise) that the concept of hearing a person's voice through the medium of a telephone must have been thought of as a supernatural pipe-dream. Now we have the technology not only to speak with anybody in the world (or in space) but also we can send documents to them through telefax. Can anyone doubt for a minute that there will be further developments in this line, maybe facilitating our contact with worlds we can currently only reach through the medium of specially gifted people? There are those who claim this has already been achieved – and I refer those interested to John G. Fuller's work, *The Ghost of 29 Megacycles*.*

Before moving on to the final stages of the preparatory process, perhaps it is as well to mention one final caveat in respect of making the appointment. If your proposed consultant asks you any more

* Fuller writes about the pioneering work of George Meek, who was previously an engineer and has developed instruments for reception of paranormal voices, particularly the "Spiricom". Earlier research done in this field is reported in Konstantin Raudive's book, *Breakthrough, an Amazing Experiment in Electronic Communication with the Dead* (Colin Smythe, Gerrards Cross 1971).

questions than the very basic ones of name, telephone contact number and (in the case of astrologers) area of interest (to establish what type of astrological chart you want), then you may need to think twice about your choice. Genuine people in this field tend to ask as few personal questions as possible, because the information you give them might actually confuse them.

Preparing Your Material

Before the consultation you will need to consider very carefully what it is you want to ask. Although one matter may be uppermost in your mind (the reason for seeking the consultation) it is amazing how the importance of this can get out of proportion, occasioning you to forget to ask about other important issues for which you could have got guidance, had you asked. When I look back on my notes of past consultations, I find that the matter then uppermost in my mind can appear incredibly minor, months or even weeks after the reading. Of course this is not always so, but it is as well to prepare several subsidiary questions in case information about your key question is not forthcoming, or in case other information you receive during the reading raises associated issues. Consider all angles, and include a question or two about those who are close to you. Sometimes information about them gives a clear indication of what *your* place might be in the future scheme of things!

Having said that, some foretellers will not answer questions about other people. They feel it is an invasion of privacy. You can only try, and if you get put off, do not be offended.

It is a good idea to write down your main lines of enquiry beforehand so that you can refer to them during the consultation. It is amazing how sessions of this kind can distract from the most fundamental issues.

Consulting Mediums

If you are thinking of consulting a medium it is as well to know that they are a special case in that their primary function is not to foretell the future but to contact people you knew who have died.

As such special questions should be prepared for them, although whether you will have them answered is another matter! Consultations with mediums are possibly the most challenging, emotionally draining, and yet tremendously reassuring (of the continuity of life after death) of the ESP techniques but are not to be taken on by the faint-hearted. Much of the work of spiritualist churches is to do with mediums, to pass messages of this kind on to their congregation, and much of the poor reputation psychic work has gained in the past has come from this source, not always warranted (occasioned largely because of the difficulty of relaying messages to the appropriate person in a large congregation).*

A medium should always try to put you in touch with somebody who was close enough to you in life to provide you with irrefutable evidence of who they are – and hopefully to give you good advice as well, sometimes even to tell you something about your future. But because of the – dare we say – "unpredictable" element of sittings with mediums, you cannot do more than prepare a speculative list of questions: for nobody knows who is going to "come through". So try to select questions which could only be answered by the subjects you have in mind.

In my experience of genuine mediumship, evidence will be provided without your seeking it, as proof of identity of the discarnate soul is of prime importance. A very numinous example of this happened to me on the very first occasion that my father "came through". He told me of a rosebush he and my mother had planted before my birth in our family home in Australia. At the time I was impatient with such information which I felt to be irrelevant as well as time-wasting! However, looking back I can now see that he wanted to tell me something which could only be substantiated by the third person (my mother), thus proving that it was not being "read", that is, telepathised from my mind. This is the best of all evidence.

* Well-known medium Owen Potts has said that when he did mediumistic work in spiritualist churches he was always shown a little blue light above the head of a person for whom a message was directed: however he found it extremely difficult on occasions to detect among the rows of heads, exactly which head the light indicated.

Penultimate Preparations

As you approach the day of your sitting, especially if it is your first, you may find yourself experiencing a conflicting cocktail of sensations – apprehension, doubt, excitement and cynicism. It is important that you try to let go and trust in the future, because your attitude will definitely have an effect on the end result. It has been observed for many years that psychic experiments do not seem to go well in the presence of sceptics. At first scientists who were witnessing abortive attempts to repeat psychic experiments contended that this was further proof of their invalidity. Now quantum physics has shown that the observer definitely does affect the observed, and in the subtle-energy level at which psychics work (some of them actually describe its energy field as a vastly speeded up vibrational plane of communication) it must be obvious that good results depend on everything going for them, not against. Which is why I have made an attempt to identify all of the seemingly minor issues which together could influence the results. The more that can be eliminated, the better. Scientists often put psychic experimentees into Faraday cages in order to screen out all other radio and electromagnetic fields which may interfere with their receptivity (also to ensure they cannot cheat!) but in the final analysis their results can still be affected by negative thinking.

The positive attitude required is not, as some scientists think, naïve and ingenuous. Once the information has come across, it can always be tested empirically for validity (which is the only test the seeker ever needs), but until and unless it does reach the consultant it cannot be tested for anything. Having an open mind is not synonymous with gullibility.

On the day before your appointment, your final plans must be made. You may or may not deem it wise to telephone the consultant to re-establish the appointment and you may or may not deem it necessary to get final directions.

If you are going to use a tape recorder, set aside two tapes, and if you have them, two recorders. Take a notebook as well with your questions in it. The reason for all this "i" dotting and "t" crossing is that every now and then, recorders play up and refuse to function in the presence of some psychics. One well-known medium told me there were days when it happened, apparently without reason, interspersed with long periods when it did not. There is much we do not know about this work, and all we can do is try and cover all contingencies. On two or three occasions it has happened to me, that I have not got anything on the tape, and I have been glad of my braces-and-belt notes taken during the session. I prefer to use tape recorders with *new* batteries and not rely on the power supply of my expert, as many of them have wiring (and plugs) which should be in museums. These people do not always live in the twentieth century; in fact one famous Tarot-card reader told me that she spent most of her time, when she wasn't giving readings, in the sixteenth century! Since we are told by scientists that time travel is only around the next but one corner, I no longer laugh at her remark, which was made in all seriousness.

One other vital issue has to be decided and that is your preference for attending your session alone or accompanied. Some people feel understandably anxious and like to have somebody around them, but do bear in mind that if you decide to have a friend or relative accompany you, that person will want to know ALL when you emerge!

Over the years I have come to the conclusion that each must make his own decision based on personality needs, but there is one golden NO and that is taking with you anybody who might play a major role in the substance of your reading. One clear advantage of deciding to have a companion is that they can drive you home, because your perceptions will be altered for a few hours at least by the process of the consultation and you will not have your mind on anything mechanical. So unless your car knows its own way home (metaphorically speaking) you are advised not to take it.

Before your reading try to keep events and traumas out of your life. Give yourself a chance to be presented in the best possible light, minus drugs or alcohol. In so doing we encourage the foretellers to concentrate on major issues, not transient afflictions. (One psychic I visited after enjoying a particularly good lunch in Brighton spent an inordinate amount of my session time telling me why I should not have eaten lobster and what I *should* be eating . . .

when all I wanted to know was if I would marry the man who had bought me the lobster!) The important thing to remember is that sensitives, in order to read for us, have to identify with us, either by holding an object belonging to us or by actually tuning in to our body and its vibrations. Hence it is extremely difficult to read for somebody who has carried an unpleasant attitude or emotion into the session room. The tendency is to "drop" the vibration of whatever they are bringing as one would drop a hot potato. Obviously people do come in distressed, but they need not come in drunk and disorderly.

I vividly remember being called in to the British Sunday newspaper *News of the World*'s offices once to analyse the handwriting of a mysterious subject about which they would tell me nothing. When I arrived a handwriting sample, closely written, was thrust into my hands and about three or four journalists crowded around me. I dropped the sample and refused to pick it up – it seemed to burn my hands. Once I had done the analysis at a distance (and told them the writer of the handwriting sample was uncontrollably violent) I discovered that I had been shown the handwriting of a mass murderer. I am not normally sensitive in this way but this incident made me realise what sensitives must suffer when they hold objects belonging to people, how they pick up health conditions, and why they need so much peace and rest in between sessions.

Summary

1. Choose your consultant according to needs. (For help consult key at the end of Chapter 2.)

2. Ask for a referral if your first choice proves abortive. (Consultants usually know who is good in their field).

3. Make your appointment, establishing date, time, length and cost of session and how payment should be made. Exchange telephone numbers and get adequate directions, including estimated time of journey.

4. Establish what you may bring in the way of tape recorders, objects belonging to yourself and others.

5. Prepare a list of questions in order of importance.

6. Decide who you are going to tell and whether you wish to be accompanied on the journey (NOT into the session).

7. Choose unpretentious clothing, preferably in a plain colour.

8. Don't eat or drink anything which could upset you or the consultant.

9. Arrive early and wait outside. BE POSITIVE!

4

THE CONSULTATION
Extracting the Information

You have arrived for your consultation, reading, sitting, session . . . call it what you will, and you have been shown into a room and asked to wait. You were on time. There doesn't seem to be anyone ahead of you – what is the problem?

The problem is that the consultant (especially if using a psychic faculty) is waiting for your vibrations to settle down. You have come in from travel, from the street, and your subtle body or aura, the electromagnetic field which surrounds your solid body like a two- to three-foot-wide invisible gaseous sheath (denser nearer the body, wispier further away) has not yet composed itself.* So the consultant simply waits until you have settled into your environment and directed your mind towards the reason for being there.

Of course there are also very mundane reasons as to why you may be kept waiting, none of them to do with your aura. In the twenties and thirties when a different kind of "fortune-telling" was in vogue, it was customary for a lot of trappings to surround the reading – it was thought to add atmosphere to the occasion. Hence the querent was often kept waiting for a bit so that the medium could make a grand entrance. There are still tiny traces of this in the attitudes of some mediums and psychics, probably because their knowledge has been handed down (these gifts are often inherited) and they have observed their elders in the field behaving in a certain way. Whatever the reason, if you are kept waiting, try to wait patiently. You are, after all, a "patient" of a kind.

---

* Books on the aura are to be found at the end of Chapter 8.

27

The Process and its Nature

When the consultant comes in, let him or her take control. Set up your tape recording equipment, get out your notebook, but otherwise keep your profile low. The consultant may tell you what process the reading will take, and many of them preface their work by either a prayer or mantra, or by delivering a little homily about how they work and what might happen and what not.

After that there will be a period while they compose their thoughts, and this can be a several-minutes' silence if a medium or psychic is tuning in to another wave-length. Try not to distract them – it is a bit like tuning in the crystal of old radio sets.

When they begin, it may well be on something least important. That is too bad. You are advised to let them get the bulk of what they have to say over before you start questioning and interrupting. However, there is one thing you need to do and it is very important: if the consultant looks to you for substantiation of a name they are getting or to know whether a piece of information has relevance to you, you must claim it if you recognise it. And my advice is, even if you do not immediately recognise its relevance to you, do not deny it out-of-court. Simply say that you cannot place it at this moment. Odds are you may recall it later, but you will (or may) discourage the consultant if you categorically disclaim something.

There is a delicate balance to be struck here between supporting the consultant through his/her endeavours and not letting the cat out of the bag and telling all about your life. Striking this balance is one of the keys to the success of your reading. Too much substantiation of facts coming to light becomes distorting information – as unwelcome to the genuine expert as it is to you, but too little support and substantiation can have a dampening effect. So answer simple questions just as you would answer them to your doctor – after all, nobody expects a doctor to work out what is wrong with you without eliciting some symptoms from you!

In the case of consultants working on a non-ESP level (if there *is* such a level in this field) you will need to give them correspondingly more help. Astrologers, for example, need to know whether events they are describing (or character traits) are known to you and whether they have relevance. They tend to work more in the dialogue mode, almost like a counsellor or psychologist works. Tarot-card readers do much the same: they will want to know if you are familiar with the fair-haired man of doubtful morals that they think may be courting you, or the child who is a bit wayward, etc.

The details of how each method works are in the next section of the book, but each type of reading has its own process, a structure which the consultant uses in order to extract information relevant to you. It is in some cases almost a ritual. But before you begin to feel discomfort about this think about the many rituals that go on in the Christian Church – the lighting of the altar candles, the taking of communion, the process of prayer itself. When we are accustomed to something it becomes natural, when we are not it becomes supernatural, and we start to suspect or even to fear something which is simply unfamiliar.

Some astrological consultants will give you a beautifully-drawn chart to look at while they are doing your reading; others will work from an unintelligible computer print-out. Some Tarot-card readers will ask you to select every one of the cards they lay, others will barely ask you to touch them. Palmists may merely glance at your hand, or ask to hold it, or they may take prints and mark and measure every major line with a millimetre scale. Some may begin by paying attention to the method they use (the palm, the runes, stones, sticks, etc) and then go off into a kind of reverie, losing all apparent interest in their method. Theirs is the reason why, not yours. Results are all that matters. So do not become over-involved in the technique used, such as what cards have been laid for you, for example, and whatever you do, do not try to get a record of them to look up for yourself afterwards. They are the tools for that day, and like the weather, they will change tomorrow.

The Questioning Process

There will come a time in the reading when you sense a change of pace. Major issues will have been brought to light, and now the minor ones begin to surface. This is the time to ask your questions, to direct the rest of the conversation into an avenue of exploration which you do want. There is usually such a wealth of information available to any client (certainly in astrology and in palmistry) that you need to decide where your main area of interest lies. To have done that right from the start of the reading, however (unless the consultant asks you or has asked you when making the appointment), is to take the risk of not hearing some piece of information which you never dreamed was in the offing and which is extremely relevant indeed.

When you start asking your questions, you may find that the consultant will move into a different mode, almost into a counselling mode. It is very important to assess this information later and to decide whether it was just a wise person giving you advice or whether fresh and further information was brought to light on your problem which, although it constitutes advice, does nevertheless come from a source other than opinion. You may well decide that the opinions of your consultant are worthy of note anyway, but this is a distinction which needs to be made. All of us, myself included, have influenced this stage of the proceedings, and in retrospect it is clear that our personal desires can influence the consultant to change an initial comprehension of a matter.

Here is an example: a man once went to a clairvoyant because he had been offered a key job but he was uncertain whether to take it. He had been ill and he knew that the newly-offered job contained similar elements of pressure to his last job which he had left due to the illness. However it was so "right" for him and so timely that he was tempted.

The consultant began the reading (without being told his purpose for seeking it) by telling him that she could see him walking down a road and that the sun was coming up – a good sign, she said. Then she elaborated by suggesting that the next three months would be *a preparation period*, after which he would be offered work "which would exactly suit his current needs and desires". She suggested that things would dramatically improve by the end of that period and that he would feel better in health too.

When the time came for questions he told her about his new job offer and pressed her to give an opinion. She hesitated. "Well," she said, "I know things are going to get better for you *very soon* and part of that improvement is a job offer. I *saw* it; but as for *now* . . ." A short discussion ensued and together they decided he should go for the job. He did and had a relapse which put him back nearly three months, during which time the new job was not kept open for him. Exactly three months after his appointment with the consultant, however, he was offered another job much more to his liking and with much less pressure.

Who was wrong? Only their compromise was wrong. If they had examined the images together of the sun coming up and the three-month waiting period they would have realised that the images were suggesting it was the *dawn* of a new era for him, not its high noon, as the timing of the first job offer might have suggested. That the clairvoyant was less to blame than her client I am in little doubt, because she had probably half-forgotten what she had told him earlier – such information comes from an evanescent source and returns there once it has been given to the recipient, because it has no relevance to the clairvoyant whatsoever. Unlike the astrological consultant or the palmist who takes prints (that is, records) she will not make, or keep, notes. Some do not even remember clients from one visit to the next. Others vaguely remember faces, but the circumstances for which the client consulted them leave them once the client walks out of the door. Frankly, if they do not, then it is a waste of time ever returning to that source of information again, because any future information will be distorted by what they remember about you, or worse, by their expectations of what they told you the last time.

Methods of Working

A word needs to be added here about the very different way in which psychics and non-psychics work in respect of the consultation process. Although, as I have said, it is difficult to separate psychic faculties entirely from this field, there are those who clearly work exclusively with them and those who work predominantly with other techniques, such as astrology, palmistry and graphology. The latter are semi-sciences, in that a body of knowledge has to be learned in order to practise them. People in these fields tend to give more structured, "of this world" type of readings in which the consultative and counselling aspect is a focal, if not predominant aspect. (This does not mean they cannot predict the future for you, but they do so in a different way.)

When you go for sittings of this nature you can expect that notes will be taken and material built up over the years. In a way you could say that these techniques and those who practise them work on form in much the same way as does a stock exchange analyst or a racing tipster, where the building up of records and the consulting of them at a later date can be a distinct advantage.

The psychic (medium, psychometrist, crystal-ball gazer, Tarot-card reader, geomancer, etc) works in a completely different mode. They work on impressions and information received from sources extraneous to those mental processes which we have come to accept as the norm, such as thinking, deduction, logic, even intuition, and from the five senses. They work from sources not available to the average person, sources gained through extra-sensory perception (ESP) or what is commonly called the sixth sense. As such their information is not logged in the same way, nor should it be. In fact it is only recently that psychics have been prepared to let people tape their readings and basically they have been goaded into this by the general public and by the scientific preoccupation of our day with evidence.

Your Part in the Procedure

Basically your reading should be conducted as a movable feast with the emphasis on flexibility – your flexibility. The more open-minded you are, the more accepting of both the method and the delivery and even of information which may seem initially incredible, the more you are likely to get out of your experience, both in terms of information and in terms of advice. I can recall many occasions when clients have stared at me incredulously as I have suggested some event which I see in their future, or even some event which I have seen in their past, and I used to be very put off by their incredulity, especially if describing an event in their past! And on just as many occasions I have been telephoned days, weeks or even months later by clients saying, "I've just remembered! We *did* have a gardener called Fred and he *did* save my life when I jumped into the river fully clad" ... and so on. And the same happens with clients who are told events they will not believe about their future. They come round to it in the end but meanwhile they could have undermined the confidence of their consultant and hence adversely affected the results.

Wrapping it Up

Once the consultant has indicated that the reading is over, you are advised to leave promptly. You may be fascinated, even enchanted (there is nothing more enchanting than information about yourself and your future possibilities!) but to the expert you are just another (albeit valued) client in her very ordinary world – ordinary because she has come to accept gifts and talents which others regard as extraordinary as being part and parcel of her life.

When you are out on the street, congratulate yourself. You have taken a courageous step, the first step down the long road to changing your future – for the better, of course. Because you will be making informed choices.

Now your only problem is ... who to tell!

Summary

1. Co-operate but do not collaborate with your consultant.

2. Respect your consultant's methods, no matter how quaint or superfluous they may seem.

3. Try to stay on the positive side of neutral as and when you are told things even if you do not immediately recognise their relevance to you. Confirm briefly those which you do see as relevant but do not offer elaboration.

4. Allow the main flow of the reading to pass with as few interruptions as seem feasible. The keyword at this stage is *listen*.

5. When the pace slackens ask relevant questions, but do not persist or press a matter if the answer seems not to be forthcoming –

although you may consider approaching the matter from a different angle. (The important thing is not to argue with the consultant but to ask for elaboration if a direction is obscure.)

6. Take notes all the way through, especially of anecdotal material and graphic descriptive phrases. These may not have relevance now, but they may flash into your consciousness later and you will realise their significance.

7. When the consultation is over, leave promptly, without post mortems. (You do not want the consultant to remember you and your "case"; you want them to forget so that they will approach you afresh next time.)

8. In your excitement, do not forget to pay!

5
THE AFTERMATH
Processing and Applying the Information

With your consultation over, you now have a body of knowledge to draw on concerning yourself, some of which may have highlighted personal traits and aspects you did not know existed, relating not only to your future, but also to your past. Going to an expert who turns the spotlight on you like this is a bit like catching a glimpse of yourself in a mirror at an angle not customarily used.

Some parts of what you have been told may have enchanted you – you cannot get them out of your head. Others may have confounded you or even filled you with apprehension. You will tend to remember the bits you want to remember and, after a day or so, completely forget some of the more "foreign-sounding" bits or some of the bits with less meaning.

This is a danger, because it is often those bits which crop up as events in your life at a later stage, giving you a sense of déjà vu but none the less catching you unawares when you could and should have been prepared. Hence it is important to listen to the tape you have taken immediately after your session and to make notes of the topics discussed. Put them under headings: *personal, health, job, money, family,* and last but not least, *timing of events.*

The reason for doing this is two-fold: firstly there is every likelihood that you will not have time to play that tape again for a while (in fact, after the first few times, you should not do so for at least six months) and secondly you need to have what has been said in black and white, at your elbow, because otherwise there is a danger that the whole episode will become like a dream in your memory. In a way the consultant has tapped that self-same part of your unconscious (which knows all things about your past, present and future) and thus it is from the same source as dreams arise that the information has come. (Does this surprise you? Think about it. Think about the times you have said, "I never dreamed I'd do so-and-so ..." or "I never dreamed I'd see *him* again!" These are all phrases which not only describe drawing on the unconscious but also infer that therein lies an information-source to our future.) Many cultures both explore and exploit their dreams for this reason (see Chapter 15).

Having made your master list, it is now important to analyse it, and to categorise it in this sort of way:

(*a*) Completely new concepts about myself and my future.

(*b*) Concepts I *sort of* knew about but had not mentally crystallised into future plans and actions.

(*c*) Completely new concepts about my family/friends/others.

(*d*) Concepts I *sort of* knew concerning family/friends/others and their character/behaviour patterns but had not faced.

(*e*) Timing of moves, events, opportunities as discussed.

This last category is of great importance and may require some work to be done on it before you can derive any reliable information about such future happenings, in order that you can sail with the tide and plan. Timing is one of the most notoriously difficult aspects of predictive work, one which catches the best psychics and astrologers out again and again, usually because subjective judgment interferes with the objective process, either from the client or from the expert.

Yet it is one of the most vital aspects of your reading, for if you are really honest with yourself, you know that you sought your consultation in order to find out what would happen in the future and not about the many other things which the expert concentrated upon. Furthermore, it is future predictions and information which test the validity of the whole process, enabling us to believe that there *is* a pattern, that certain things *are* meant (no matter how difficult it may be for us to understand them at the time) and that we *can* take charge of our future and not leave it, as we are wont, in the hands of others who may like to influence it in ways to suit themselves, rather than ourselves – human nature being what it is!

So you must try to find as many clues in your reading as you can about the timing and solidity of events which have been predicted. You may not succeed but it is worth the try.

Let us take some examples and firstly a very simple one. This actually happened to a friend of mine – in fact, all the examples in this book are taken from actual experiences. My friend went to see a psychic who told her that she would be moving home, in fact that she could see her with her little girl walking up the path to the home she would eventually choose – and that as she did so there would be a smell of hyacinths around the door.

Some years later my friend was looking for a home. She wanted one in a certain area but did not think she could afford it. Nevertheless she decided to look at one house in that area because it particularly appealed to her. As she walked up the path with her little girl she smelled hyacinths, and suddenly she remembered the words of the psychic.

She bought the house and twenty-five years later is still happy in it. However, she says that she would never have entered into negotiations (which were difficult and daunting) had she not "known in her heart" that the house was for her because of what the psychic had said. This is where help of this kind can be immeasurable: in enabling people to separate the wheat of their possibilities from the chaff of their impossibilities, because both can look very much the same when one is in the middle of making choices!

Analysing that story further is interesting: firstly, the only clue to timing was in fact a clue to the *season* in which she would buy the house – the hyacinth season. (Note that in the prediction she was walking up the path when she smelt the hyacinths, which indicated they were growing *outside*, not inside.)

Secondly, the prediction had no clue to the *year* in which the transaction might take place. This is the maddening aspect of a great deal of this work. Unless there was some other piece of information contained in the psychic's vision of my friend walking up that path, that was all she had to go by. But imagine if my friend had thought to ask the psychic, "How old does my little girl look?" Or: "Can you see what my little girl is wearing?" Children grow quickly, and if the dress described had been familiar to my friend, then she could have presumed that the event might take place in the ensuing hyacinth season.

Hopefully this simple incident with its extensions into possible lines of questioning will aid you in your understanding of how to question psychics when they have visions of your future and how to look for substantiation of the timing of events. Of course you cannot interrupt them at every moment of your reading, but if there is a pause or an opening, and if a question pops into your mind about something they have seen, then it is just possible that they may not have described to you the whole of their vision and to encourage them to do so may clarify matters for you.

After the event, of course, you can only analyse what you already have, and one of the reasons why this particular discourse has been included in the aftermath and not in the preparation chapters is because it is necessary to have had an experience yourself, with data known and personal to you, before you can begin to understand how you may constructively intervene in and clarify events described in future readings.

The acquisition of knowledge about your future should not be thought of as a rare-occasion event, to be repeated only when you are at a crossroads (when it is often too late), but something you should envisage incorporating into your life conceivably on an annual basis with possibly two or three experts who use completely different techniques. In that way a mosaic can be built up and cross-checking of events predicted can lead to better substantiation.

So you would be advised to analyse your first attempt at acquiring knowledge of this kind with a view to learning from your mistakes as much as for collecting data. Meanwhile you have started to influence your future from a position of some knowledge – that in itself is an achievement.

Language Difficulties

Sometimes you may experience difficulties with the language or terminology or, even more abstruse, the symbolism used by the experts you visit.

Language difficulties are usually caused by the pictorial, at times old-fashioned way in which much of this information comes through, especially if ESP faculties have been used. Psychics tend to say things like: "I am being shown a gown ... I think it is a bridal gown ... does this mean anything to you? ... and at the same time I am being shown a young woman at a gateway and she is hesitating ... ah ... there's another person involved who's all at sea ... or is he *away* at sea ... can you place this one?"

This is a classic example of a psychic needing the helpful clarification mentioned in Chapter 4 – something like "yes, yes, I know her" or "yes, there is a sailor involved" – not giving too much away but prompting a line of enquiry. And yet this sort of language can be very misleading: the psychic may not actually give you alternative versions of her image – for example, she may have stopped with "he's all at sea ..." so it is up to you (the querent) afterwards to go through the imagery used and see what *you* can make of it. For example: "Is there a gate or gateway I particularly remember, and if so what was I doing at the time? What was I thinking or feeling – is it perhaps the same sort of feeling?"

Symbolism is even more difficult. On the rare occasion it can be easy, such as the occasion when I was told by a clairvoyant that he saw the American flag waving above my head for a second. (I did make a key journey to America shortly afterwards.) But when it is something archetypal in nature, of the stuff that dreams are made (and the symbols are very similar and seem to cross the boundaries of race, culture, language, and be common to all mankind), then help is sometimes needed with their interpretation.

For this purpose a book of symbols is a useful tool, and one or two titles are suggested at the end of Chapter 8, on ESP, where the universal language of symbols is further explored.

Sometimes (and astrologers are particularly guilty of this) the language of the technique of foretelling intrudes, such as, "Well, with Sun conjunct Pluto what can you expect? ..." Or, "I see you've got Venus square Mars natally – how DO you get on with the opposite sex?" Implying you *should* know all about it. Whereas one can hardly ask a psychic to stop having visions in symbols, one can certainly ask an astrologer to speak in one's own language, which is why a follow-up telephone session with all experts excepting those incorporating ESP (who will not remember) is advised, during which (having made notes) you can ask them to clear up anything you do not fully understand.

Sharing the Information

Your future is something intensely personal to you and experience may teach you (too late in some cases) to keep it to yourself. However if you do decide to confide in someone the time to do it is now, before the predictions have had time to come to pass. That way you will have a second source of confirmation when and if something happens. Also, the person you tell will probably remember things differently from you and may remind you when a situation crops up about which you have been told something.

Fate or Free Will ... Can We Choose?

Fate does not keep road-menders on her highways. Oscar Wilde
Free will is the right to do gladly that which I know I must do. C. G.
Jung.

Sooner or later you are bound to enter into a dialogue, with either yourself or others, about whether we can change our future by studying its projected options or not. Any opinion on this subject can only be hypothetical, but from my observation of clients over the years I have come to believe that not everything in life is "written in the stars". We do seem to have a measure of free-will, but equally do I contend that we have a measure of fate to deal with as well. It seems that there are times in life when we have important options presented to us and some of those options are looser (that is, we have more freedom of choice in them) than others. In some major respects (the milestones of life) we do not appear to have so much room for choice – key relationships, for example, can seem inevitable – we cannot *not* go through with them. Whereas other options seem to have wider room for choice, and it is those mini-milestones in our lives which we can perhaps influence more than the others, so it helps to know in advance about them.

Of course there are alternative viewpoints: two extremes of which are (*a*) that we have no choice at all, which is a view largely Eastern in origin or (*b*) the predominantly Western view that we are the architects of our future and that there is no such thing as karma, fate, destiny, events which are pre-ordained, or anything of that nature. Perhaps the nearest we can come to equating all these points of view is to suggest that *character is destiny*. And if that is the case, the more we know of ourselves and the more we understand our character and its innate potential, the better can be our destinies.

There does seem to be one other key factor in the executing of destiny and that is environmental. This is best illustrated by the parable of the seed. A very interesting illustration of this occurred in the reign of English King Charles II. It was noted that a son was born to a commoner working in the Court on the same day and at almost exactly the same time as the birth of the King. On the day the King was crowned the commoner's son began his very first job: on the day the King married, the commoner's son married, and they both died on the same day. However, the difference between their lifestyles was as chalk to cheese: one had been given every opportunity to prosper, the other not. This example classically illustrates the tight-option/loose-option hypothesis as well, since the milestones of birth, work, marriage and death were unchanged by birth or circumstance.

The fate versus free-will debate has been waged over the aeons of foretelling. I prefer to think of life as having a general curriculum, which sets out guidelines as to what must be learned, but leaves the fine print to the student.

Summary

1. Listen to the tape-recording of your session and combine it with the notes you have taken in order to make a clear, brief record of the salient points, especially where the timing of future events is concerned.

2. Start analysing and sifting through what you have been told – but do not act immediately unless you are absolutely sure. Try to make sense of any allegorical language, with the help of a book of symbols if necessary.

3. Consider what your next step should be (for example, discussing moves with a trusted friend, having a follow-up session with your consultant on the telephone, getting an entirely different opinion, going to see a counsellor, expressing dissatisfaction, etc).

Booklist

The best book to help with the interpretation of symbols is, to my mind, *An Illustrated Encyclopaedia of Traditional Symbols* by J. C. Cooper, Thames & Hudson, London, 1978, 1982, 1988.

6
YOUR NEXT STEP?

You have now absorbed your reading, classified the data, told everyone you are going to tell and are currently in the position where, for the first time in your life, you actually have memories of your future! What to do about those "memories" and how much to allow them to influence your ongoing plans, options and decisions, must now become a crucial issue.

But let us first look more deeply at whether your memories are largely of a positive nature or quite the reverse. Readings have climates which tend to presage the climate of the times you are about to enter. If you are about to enter a "summer" period of your life when all is advancement and light, your reading will probably have uplifted you and inspired you to get on. Your only danger will be if you imagine it will all happen without your help, or else that your anticipation is so great that you virtually dwell in your future and neglect your present – the only part of your life you *can* influence.

If you are about to enter a "winter" period, such as the loss of a job, the break-up of a relationship, illness, or financial pressure, then it is unlikely that your reading will have inspired you with so much purpose and positivity, however well it has been conducted. But you have been given a valuable opportunity to prepare yourself and so long as you view what has been said as giving you a chance to do just that – to investigate alternatives or preventive moves or simply to gather strength for the inevitable – then the results can only be positive.

Getting a Second Opinion

If your reading has suggested that a major move or event is likely to develop in the future, you may be interested in getting a second opinion. Your decision to do so should be directly proportional to the severity or importance of what you have been told. If you were told by your doctor that you should have a major operation, you would consider it wise to get a second opinion, and the same law applies to foretelling, though amazingly few people even consider it. They seem to believe that their experience is so rare or so numinous that they had better not rock the boat by trying it again.

This is not only ignorant, it is ill-advised. It is not allowing the laws of common sense to enter into a field where they have not ventured for too many years. So do not hesitate to set up another consultation and do so quite quickly if there are major events predicted. It is especially advisable to do so if you feel troubled by what you have heard, especially if it arouses deep echoes from the past which make you think you have "been there before". Such a feeling suggests you may be about to repeat a pattern, and you will need to look at that pattern very closely and see if you are doing so quite unconsciously and to your own detriment. We all get programmed by our childhoods and the programmes are not always positive or appropriate to adult life. However, because a certain type of experience is familiar to us we tend to select it again and again without realising what we are doing. It is the better-the devil-you-know syndrome and psychologists are well familiar with it. If you suspect that your "other self" is playing such dirty tricks on you, you may like to consider the options mentioned later in this chapter concerning getting psychological counsel, which will help you to understand your unconscious motivations.

Who to Choose

If you decide to seek another opinion, your second choice of consultant should be governed by what type of reading you chose in the first place. Basically it should be of a completely different category, so that if your first choice was somebody with psychic ability (a medium, clairvoyant, Tarot-card reader, crystal-gazer, sand-reader, etc), you should now choose someone who works in a more "scientific" way, such as an astrologer, palmist, or graphologist. This is because they will put structure into what you have been told and you may ask them questions about your options for the future which can be discussed in a more analytical way.

Conversely, if your first choice was for one of these structured so-called "scientific" techniques, then you should choose somebody with psychic ability who will paint details into the canvas of your future possibilities.

Only under very rare circumstances should you consult someone of the same category as before and that is when you have had a traumatic reading, one you could not relate to at all, and you feel that the consultant you were unlucky enough to choose was incompetent or, worse, negligent, or even destructive. Then you should choose another in the same field, in order to compare results; openly telling them of your prior experience and raising every one of the upsetting points with them – but not, you are advised, until the second half of your consultation: wait and see what they have to tell you first, unbiased by news of your previous trauma.

Often a second consultant can allay your fears and, even if they acknowledge the validity of the first reading, offer a completely different viewpoint or solution. A great deal of my work over the years has been concerned with allaying fears raised by extreme interpretations of likely events.

If, after your second consultation, you decide that your first consultant was extremely destructive or incompetent, you may feel you owe it to the consensus of responsible and true souls who work in the same field to let your displeasure be known, either to the consultant or to their representative organisation, for example, the Astrological Association, BAPS, the British Astrological and Psychic Society, or the Graphology Society, etc or whatever seems relevant. (They are listed in Part 3.) But do think carefully about such a step, because years later you may come to realise why they may have said some of the things: however, this does not excuse the fact that their sense of timing and your readiness to understand were two areas which they did not judge correctly.

This is not to imply that dire forebodings, however unwelcome, will ultimately come true. A client of mine was once warned by a Tarot-card reader of a serious health condition (first spread of cards). In the second spread she threw caution to the winds and suggested that it was a terminal illness. In the third spread she actually designated my client's mourners – husband and son. She is still very much alive twenty years later and often jokes with me that the only terminal illness she possesses is that which carries us all off in the end – life itself!

On the vexed question of dire predictions, most experts feel that they are not only destructive, since they take away people's will to fight, but they can actually make a healthy person sicken and die. In Australia it is well known that when an aborigine "points the bone" at another in a certain will-to-death ceremony, it is only a matter of time (usually days or weeks) before the other will die – the belief in the process is so strong. The same principle, though not to such a degree, affects all human nature. Hence it must be considered malpractice to offer a dire prediction: one expert (palmist Mir Bashir) describes it this way: "We are here to help the living and our craft is directed towards considerations of life, not death."

I once interviewed a very good psychic who had a wicked sense of humour and in the course of the interview I asked him what he would say to a client if he saw death for him. He grinned. "I would tell him to prepare himself for a very big change in life!" Jokes aside, death *is* a change, an exciting one, and new evidence which has been brought to bear from those who have had near-death experiences indicates it is more like a birth (into another, better world) and absolutely not the end. But that is the subject of its own chapter, and is simply mentioned in the early part of this book to allay some of the fears which surround the possibility of receiving a negative prediction.

New Avenues of Study

You may find, as many do, that delving into your future whets your appetite for more knowledge. You may wish to understand more about yourself once part of the intriguing pattern of your life has been revealed to you. Or you may wish to understand how the experts have achieved their results – to learn the tricks of their trade.

There is little doubt that pursuits of this kind can lead you on a voyage of self-discovery, an exploration which can only benefit your future choices. The attitude to psychological counselling has changed dramatically in the last two or three decades: emphasis is now placed on self-understanding and not on relationships going wrong or other forms of crises in your life. Workshops exist which offer introductions to these sorts of explorations (some are mentioned in Part 3) and experiencing some of them may or may not lead you to pursue self-understanding with the help of a guide or counsellor. Many who do consider it the best move they ever made.

The other form of exploration which is often prompted by entering the world of the future is to actually find out how it is done and to learn a technique for yourself. There is a short do-it-yourself section in Part 2 of this book, as well as a section in Part 3 which is devoted to providing information about courses in your chosen subject, some of which can even be pursued at home by correspondence. There are often informal study groups in your own area which local lines of enquiry should reveal.* The purchase of any specialist magazine on the subject will usually yield a crop of course advertisements and there are always self-instruction books. So long as you remember that a little knowledge is a dangerous thing, such explorations can only improve your future prospects.

Letting Go

All that remains now is for you to let go of your future in favour of your present. Your brief insight has been designed to help you make the best plans you can but it is important not to let those plans become an overriding factor, influencing behaviour and adaptability. An example may help in the understanding of this concept. A young woman was once told that she would meet her prospective

* Space does not permit the publication of local addresses in Part 3, but national organisations listed there have their own referral systems, for example, the Astrological Association of the U.K. has detailed lists of local groups; the Urania Trust is also a source of such information.

husband locally while she was absorbed in reading something. She spent hours in the local library, neglecting her social life and her friends and making herself thoroughly miserable.

Inevitably her sight (which was never good) further deteriorated and she went to her local optician to see if she needed stronger glasses. She did: and it was while she was reading the test card of letters that she met (and later married) the new local optician! The irony of the situation was that she would have met him anyway on her annual sight check-up and saved herself a lot of boredom and eye-strain!

So ... having had your bird's eye view of what is around the next corner, return to your worm's eye view of the present. Prosaic it may seem in comparison, but it is the only part of your life you *can* influence.

PART TWO

7
THE PREDICTIVE TECHNIQUES:
An Introduction

Prophecy seldom profits the prophets. Peter Lee

In Part 2 we shall be reviewing a variety of techniques used today for predictive and other purposes, as well as examining their respective skills in relation to various consultancy requirements. However, it should be acknowledged from the outset that despite the fact that the talents and techniques of foretelling are far from limited to prediction (character analysis is usually accurately achieved), it is for the former purpose that nearly all consultations are sought!*

Hence it is of vital importance to ascertain how well each technique performs the task of prediction and whether such performances can justify the faith placed in them. It may also be relevant to examine what forces might be at work in prediction and whether our understanding of those could improve the performance, for the fact remains that the history of prediction has shown it to be a very hit-and-miss affair.

If we examine some of the greatest names in prediction – Nostradamus, for example, whose predictions are still read today even though he died in 1566, more than four centuries ago – we find a pattern which recurs constantly: some startlingly accurate hits and some unaccountable misses. The same is true of one of the most successful of today's predictors, Washington seeress Jeanne

---

* In fact an interesting phenomenon occurs in 90 per cent of all consultations sought, in that it is the personal detail given by foretellers to clients which convinces them that something very relevant to them is "coming through". Yet having received such often stunning evidence, they are immediately motivated towards projecting that person/situation/involvement into the future! So the process of divination usually consists of two parts: the personal-detail part and the person-into-the-future part.

Dixon, who is famous for having predicted both President and Robert Kennedy's deaths, as well as that of Martin Luther King and the suicide of Marilyn Monroe. But others of her predictions have been remarkably off-beam, especially in respect to some of the world events she has tackled. It would appear that she is more likely to be accurate when predicting for personalities than for nations; but this is not necessarily true of other predictors: Nostradamus' skill appears to be in national prediction (his "hits" include the French Revolution, the Great Fire of London, the rise of certain kings and emperors, including Napoleon and Hitler) and quite recently, in the same vein, contemporary astrologer Dennis Elwell predicted both the 1987 Zeebrugge ferry disaster and the London Underground train disaster.

So what is the nature of this alternatively sharp or blunt tool predictors wield, very often with the public on the side of their successes (everybody tends to remember the hits and to forget the misses)?

Prediction is supposed to be governed by the law of probability. Briefly that law states that the probability of an outcome depends on the ratio between the number of correct predictions to the number which may have been made. If, for example, we toss a coin, there is always a one in two chance of it coming down the way we predict it. Obviously the more chances there are involved (such as of throwing a six with dice where the odds are six to one or the throwing of two sixes where the odds are thirty-six to one, etc), the more remarkable an accurate prediction of the result becomes. This theory would appear to render the prediction of any random event a fantastically unlikely proposition, because the odds against doing so would be enormous. If the law of probability is all that operates in respect of prediction, then perhaps our beleaguered predictors deserve to have us forget their failures, for their successes become truly remarkable.

Fortunately pioneers like J. B. Rhine, of Duke University in America, initiated research in the nineteen-thirties and forties which showed beyond all doubt that the law of probability was an ass when it came to predicting the success rate of guesses made by certain talented people (those with faculty X?) in the community.

His experiments, conducted over a number of years (first with dice and later with PSI or Zener cards), showed that not only could certain people correctly guess outcomes wildly beyond chance (sometimes a million times beyond or more) but that some seemed to be able actually to influence the fall of the dice or predict the run of the cards.

The experiments revealed another interesting factor: where there was a positive belief in the results of the tests and a supportive atmosphere around the subjects being tested, the results were much better than when there was a negative, distrustful atmosphere. This is in line with the belief of myself and many other observers of the workings of this field (such as Paul Beard, former President of the College of Psychic Studies in London) that the attitude of the sitter, the client (Beard calls it the quality of their attention), does influence the result. (Beard advises "sympathy during, and judgment afterwards".)

One other interesting factor emerged from Rhine's experiments and that was that results tailed off after the guessers became tired or bored. So it would appear that not only does the quality of the attention of the people around the guessers have bearing on the results, but also the quality of the guessers' own attention. No wonder PSI experimentees perform notoriously badly in front of the scientific community! There has been some very interesting research done on the quality of attention, or in other words "state of consciousness" of those performing well in this field by the late Dr Maxwell Cade in London in the last few decades, but since his observations pertain mainly to those deploying ESP techniques, they will be discussed in that chapter.

This leaves only the factor of time to be considered and its effect on prediction. For this seems to be the other major factor (apart from content) which influences the success of predictions. In fact it seems to be the more demanding of the two, for where predictors may be right about the nature of an event likely to occur in the future – even be able to graphically describe it – the actual timing of it can be far astray.

Time and the Timing of Events

Why are time and the timing of events so difficult to pinpoint? Are the predictors getting their information from dimensions where there is no time – where time stands still – and in the translation from timeless to time they make mistakes? Or is it that the timing of events in our lives is so interdependent upon other key factors and people in our lives that the crystallisation of a key event is not easy to judge? Is it just suspended in the future, to happen "when time is ripe"?

Another theory, more supported by data and yet still inadequate, is that time does not always pass at the same rate, therefore rendering it difficult to judge.

Subjectively we do experience time passing at different rates. On occasions, and often when we are in the midst of a memorable experience, it does literally seem to stand still (people speak of the moment before the impact of an accident as being endless) and of course there are other occasions, usually when we are having another (joyful) type of experience when, literally, time flies. Our happiness, or boredom, or otherwise does seem to affect if not the actual passing of time, then certainly our perception of it. But is this as subjective as we have been taught to believe it is? We do not even age steadily: there are times when we age very quickly and others when we seem to go on the same for years. Yet we all seem to arrive at threescore and ten having experienced overall the passage of time very much the same as our neighbours, no doubt because we live in the same space-time continuum – the earth.

However even this is relative; Einstein's theory by that name has established that if we were to space-travel for a decade, we would come back younger (literally years younger) than our contemporaries on earth; the exact number of years depending on how fast our space-craft had been travelling.

Whereas before, in the days of Newton and classical physics, time was thought to be linear and consistent, Einstein's Theory of Relativity and, more latterly, quantum theory, have shown that time does vary – possibly even allowing us glimpses into the past, as well as into the future. For incredibly, quantum mechanics has shown that it is possible for a body to move *backward* in time, which means that at its most retrograde point, it will know its own future!

If this seems wildly incredible, consider how our view of things changes depending on our vantage point. Imagine you are in a helicopter engaged in traffic control and you are looking down on an intersection. Approaching the intersection are two buses, travelling at right angles to each other. They are each going at the same speed, and it becomes obvious to you that unless one of them slows down, they will crash. But the people in the buses have no awareness of this "prediction" you have made. When the crash occurs, it will come, for them, "out of the blue".

Einstein tended to think that space and time were curved. Perhaps spiralling up the curves of time enables some of us to get a bird's eye view of the others. Oddly enough, people who say they can foresee events, that is, transcend time, often talk of reaching planes of a higher rate of vibration; others talk of reaching planes where time does not exist, or where the past, present and future co-exist together. This again is a difficult concept to grasp, but we can see examples of it, at least in one aspect of time, the past, in front of us whenever we look at the stars. What we see is how they were millions of light-years ago – not how they are now. Perhaps, if we only knew where to look or what to look at, we would see the stars of the future too. Suffice it to say that our concepts of time have been sufficiently shaken up in the recent past to at least allow for the possibility that in some dimension or plane which may be accessible to those with special gifts, the outlines of our future might exist.

Cases For and Against Prediction

Is then the future written? And if it is, should we try to find out what we cannot change? Here we view the old chestnut (fate v. free will) all over again but from our more modern understanding of time. Nevertheless I still prefer to think of the future as I described it in Part 1, as being a mixture of tight and loose options, some of which we have more sway over than others. Maybe time will prove me wrong, but it certainly does support the evidence we have that predictors are not always right. Sometimes – and it does seem to be in the major events of a life or of a nation – they are seen to be startlingly right: at others their opinions seem to be little more than educated guesses based more or less on another concept presented in Part 1; that character is destiny.

Really, the picture of the hit-and-miss aspect of prediction seems to be attributable to a complex jig-saw of factors rather than one dominating factor (such as time), not the least of which could turn out to be one not hitherto considered: the lack of formal training, or a body of research to support and instruct those who do try to foretell, so that they can learn to improve their performance.

Comparing the Arts

Predictive techniques come and go as the fashions and needs of society alter. Table-turning and seances were very fashionable at the turn of this century: now a different type of mediumship altogether is practised. In ancient Babylon, foretelling from reading the livers of newly-killed animals used to be the done thing; now animal welfare would step in smartly! So in choosing the techniques featured in Part 2, I have borne in mind what foretelling techniques seem to be working now or may work well (considering the direction of research) in the near future.

Efficacy of Prediction: Techniques Compared

Whilst it is difficult, if not impossible, to compare techniques which vary so dramatically as crystallomancy (usually crystal-gazing) and graphology (the analysis of handwriting), some attempt to compare the general results achieved does throw light on success rates. And there can be little doubt that first-class psychics come out on top, by virtue of the sheer weight of detail which they can provide about people and their personal situations, and about the projecting of those situations into the future (they are seldom wrong about what will happen, but sometimes wrong about when it will happen).

They are also adept at relating a client's situation to their environment, so that if there is likely to be a government shake-up, for example, which could affect the plans of the client, the psychic can tune into that as well. This is not to suggest they have all of the answers all of the time – most psychics believe that if they are not meant to know something for karmic or other reasons pertaining to the client, then they will not be shown it. However, this does not alter the fact that a tremendous amount of information seems to be available to the ordinary client seeking it, were they only to know how (and whom) to ask.

Regrettably, top-class psychics, like the few who have kindly contributed their comments in Part 2,* are few and far between, and not all members of the public will find one near their door.†

For this reason, and for its facility in helping people to structure and plan their lives, it is probably fair to say that of all the foretelling arts, *astrology* remains the single most outstanding and consistent of them, not only from the point of view of prediction, but also for its many other uses (such as character analysis and understanding the people we live with). It is by far the most prevalent method of foretelling, the most organised and supported by teaching and professional bodies, the most networked and the most accessible to those who would seek consultations. This is not to suggest that it is perfect: not until a great deal more research is done will it even approach a consistent level of proficiency, but its facility of being a vehicle for interpreting life in all its aspects and dimensions is unsurpassed.

However there is no denying what it lacks, and because it can be learned by all and does not per se require that a psychic or intuitive faculty be possessed by its consultants, the assessment it gives can suffer from the very disability that is a feature of the age of reason which we are just transcending: an overstructured,

---

* Namely psychic and geomancer David Bingham, psychics Peter Lee, Owen Potts and David Young (Potts and Young work as mediums as well) and Tarot-card reader and psychic John Christopher Travers.

† There are more good psychics than many people realise: often working in a very modest way, without advertising and very often in a site such as the local market. I once had a superb reading from a palmist in London's Shepherd's Bush market for 50p.

didactic view of a client's life and its possibilities which does not allow either for flexibility or for quantum leaps.

The success of astrology is to my mind attributable to the fact that it has managed to combine talents which facilitate knowing oneself and others with a means for assessing the timing of events in a life. Astrology has always appealed to the rationalists because it does have a theory and a structure, but it is only now developing its transpersonal, psychological and intuitive aspects which will enable the inner purposes and timings of life to be understood along with the outer.

It is interesting to note that the other largely successful area of predictive facility lies with that loose conglomerate of talented experts who possess some form of ESP ability which they often deploy with other skills and techniques, such as astrology or the Tarot. Great prophets such as Nostradamus have come from this creative source; in his case his seership was structured by astrology, as was that of John Dee and William Lilly. (Jeanne Dixon's skill is structured by astrology and crystallomancy, Cheiro's by astrology and palmistry.)

These are the people who literally can transcend time, but by the very nature of the fact that they can unstructure time, they will always suffer from inaccuracies of grounding their predictions in the world of time, even though they do receive considerable help from being able to anchor the timing of their predictions by planetary positions or by use of a physiological pattern such as the palm, the head, or (rare now) the foot, where a map of time seems to have been incorporated into a living dimension.

Palmistry lends itself better to the assistance of prediction than almost any of the aforementioned physiological patterns, since a map of the life and its major milestones does appear on the hand, with its own timing which can be judged from several lines. The problem is one of popularity: whereas astrology has prospered, palmistry has not, and good palmists are few and far between. (Here I speak of true palmistry (cheirology) and not cheiromancy, which is simply an ESP technique in which the hand is used as the focus but the lines are not read or measured.)

Graphology, the analysis of handwriting, makes no claims whatsoever in the area of prediction, except of course in support of the principle that character is destiny, and since character is so clearly evident from a study of handwriting as well as underlying psychological factors, a good graphologist could certainly make predictions based on character and ability. Graphology's true value lies in that first and most essential factor of divination, the factors most succinctly expressed by the admonition "know yourself" – the implication being that in so doing you will know others and therefore know what each is likely to do.

Phrenology can do much the same as palmistry, though regrettably without its access to a system for timing, but again it suffers even more acutely from the lack of contemporary following which besets palmistry. This is a classic example of how a technique can unaccountably lose favour: in the last century phrenology enjoyed more public (and scientific) support than any of the other devotions based on the physiological patterns. However, I predict its revival due to modern research increasingly showing interest in its tenets. Though when such a revival comes, it will probably be under the aegis of modern medicine.*

The Tarot, Cards, Runes, Sand, Crystals, etc.

Systems such as these which depend on a psychic faculty to interpret are in effect being used as a focus for psychic perception. As such their predictive and other efficacies depend almost entirely on the skill of the operator. This is why material derived from such sources can be so widely divergent in content, bearing little or no reference to the means by which the information was gleaned. And this is why rationalists who examine this area of prediction find it so impossible to accept what is predicted because they are trying to understand it on their (deductive mode) terms: for example, if the reader is using the Tarot, how has he/she arrived at the predictions given? They want to see a step-by-step translation of the meanings of the cards laid to the interpretations given for the future. This

---

* See Chapter 13. (The mapping of the zones of the head and of thought activity – consciousness – by the SQUID suggests this link. See p65.)

completely ignores the quantum leap of the reader's imagination, the selective exercise of the reader's intuitive faculty, that intrinsic "knowing" that exists at this level of the work. I challenge rationalists to recall one of those moments in their own lives when they have experienced this kind of "knowing": perhaps a moment when they "knew" that their wife/husband was lying, or a beloved pet was dying, or that all was not well with a child – and that this is probably one of the few times they have been in touch with a faculty which foretellers use all the time.

The Pros and Cons of Prediction

All people predict, not just professional foretellers. Consider the following remarks:

DOCTOR (*Overheard talking to patient from surgery door*): "If you continue to drink and smoke to this extent, I predict you will end up with coronary heart disease." (The laws of probability are on his side, but not inevitability.)

JUDGE (*Heard while doing jury duty*): "I can safely predict that you have not heard the end of this." (Neither had the criminal upon whose behaviour the judge was applying not the law of the land but the law of probability.)

WEATHER FORECASTER (*Heard while it was actually raining outside*): "An analysis of the cloud formations over Britain indicates that the weather will be fine all today and tomorrow." (And this despite their having one of the biggest computers for analysing probabilities in the British Isles.)

All these predictions were based on probability, and as we have seen, this method of predicting has limitations.

The Danger of Prediction

There is no doubt that a very strong case can be made against predictions in any form, whoever makes them. In my experience it matters little who does the predicting: doctor, lawyer, foreteller, if they contain within them a threat or warning, they will have a long-lasting effect on the subject. This is probably one of the single most important reasons why the professional standard of foretellers should be improved, their training standardised (as much as training in this area ever can be) and that such training should incorporate something akin to the medical profession's Hippocratic Oath, that is, a code of ethics to guide the nature of the advice given. I also believe, however, that the public should, with full knowledge of the ramifications, have access to information about their future, good, bad and indifferent. So improved understanding would seem to be necessary on both sides of the consulting table, and a flexible structure introduced which will in effect contain (and acknowledge) warnings. (It is only fair to add that those with true gifts in the predictive field have usually perfected them through great effort and soul-searching and have long since developed their own personal code of ethics. The difficulty lies with the second order of consultants, whose deficiency in talent is often matched by a corresponding lack of scruples.)

There is another view of this issue, however, and I think it is essential to present it. Whilst ideally there seems to be a need for improved standards and vigilance among the foretelling community, it could equally be argued that taking them under an invigilating umbrella may serve to destroy the very thing which they are offering, which is an alternative view from that which the Establishment offers. There are alarming signs of how this invigilating principle, itself a good principle in theory, is none the less threatening and affecting the practice of natural medicine today, and of alternative healing therapies, due to the projected controlling of their activities under the E.E.C. umbrella and its rules. Gifted individuals have always operated outside the Establishment and it has been from that source that nearly all progress has been made.

Possibly a compromise should be attempted, but slowly: beginning with techniques such as graphology (which is already assuming a structured professional role in modern society and is being increasingly taught in universities), followed by astrology and by any foretelling technique in which a body of knowledge is required in order to function optimally at other levels, such as the intuitive level.

This would leave the gifted fringe to function according to the laws of supply and demand. To a better informed public with greater expectations of results, this may be all that is necessary.

Prediction Upheld

Because of our obsession with the future, whether we like some of its effects or not, prediction is probably here to stay. And it does have a very positive face. Peter Lee, a gifted psychic practising in London, has said: "Besides being useful to people it is a dramatic way of proving the reality of the psychic world." Other psychics cite the raising of hopes as being one of the single most important functions of this work – this is the other side of the coin of negative prediction. Others (astrologers in particular) talk about reassuring clients when troubles (cycles) will end (which can be very helpful if you are in a bad patch and cannot see when the light is going to shine at the end of the tunnel). Predictors can also give positively angled warnings – warnings which incorporate the discussion of evasive tactics and (a little-understood aspect of their work) they can help clients to release pent-up emotions and discuss their innermost fears.

Owen Potts, another talented medium and psychic working in London, believes that all psychic work is healing, that love is the link between the seeker and the sought. If that is the case, possibly the only code of ethics needed in this mutable field would be the one advocated by Saint Augustine: "Love, and then what you will, do."

Booklist

Ebon, M. *Prophecy in our Times.* Wilshire Publishers, USA.
Feller, W. *An Introduction to Probability Theory and its Application.* New York 1968.
Gilchrist, G. *The Search for Meaning.* Dryad Press, London 1987.
Greenhouse, H. *Premonitions – A Leap into the Future.* Turnstone Press, London 1972.

Lethbridge, E. *ESP: Beyond Time and Distance.* Routledge, London 1965.

Moss, T. *The Probability of the Impossible.* New American Library, New York 1974.

Nostradamus, M. *The Prophecies of Nostradamus.* Crown Publishers Inc., New York 1970.

Rhine, J. B. *The Reach of the Mind.* Pelican Books, London 1954.

Vaughan, A. *Patterns of Prophecy.* Turnstone Press, London 1974.

8
ONE SENSE AHEAD
The Deployment of ESP in Foretelling

*The whole history of scientific advance is full of scientists investigating
phenomena that the Establishment did not believe were there.*
Margaret Mead

An article called "Boom Times on the Psychic Frontier" (published
in 1974) in *Time Magazine* contained the following introduction:

> For all the enormous achievements of science in posting the
> universe that man inhabits, odd things keep slipping past the
> sentries. The tap on the shoulder may be fleeting, the brush
> across the cheek gone sooner than it is felt, but the momentary
> effect is unmistakable: an unwilling suspension of belief in the
> rational. An old friend suddenly remembered, and as suddenly
> the telephone rings and the friend is on the line. A vivid dream
> that becomes the morning reality. The sense of bumping into
> oneself around the corner of time, of having done and said just
> this, in this place, once before in precisely this fashion. A stab
> of anguish for a distant loved one, and next day, the telegram.
>
> Hardly a person lives who can deny some such experience,
> some such seeming visitation from across the psychic frontier.
> For most of man's history these intrusions were mainsprings of
> action, the very life of Greek epic and biblical saga, of mediaeval
> tale and Eastern chronicle. Modern science and psychology have
> learned to explain much of what was once inexplicable, but
> mysteries remain. The workings of the mind still resist rational
> analysis; reports of psychic phenomena persist. Are they all
> accident, illusion? Or are there other planes and dimensions of
> experience and memory? Could there be a paranormal world
> exempt from known natural law?

Both in America and abroad these questions are being asked by increasing numbers of laymen and scientists hungry for answers. The diverse manifestations of interest in so-called psychic phenomena are everywhere.*

In publishing this lengthy article *Time Magazine* was acknowledging the step-up in the degree of interest and pace of progress of investigations into psychic matters which has been gathering strength for the past two decades.

Recent History of ESP

The seventies saw many such changes in man's fundamental attitude to matters he could not explain by scientific means: quite simply the weight of evidence of their existence became too great to ignore. Also equipment began to be built which could actually detect subtle energy fields around living objects (akin to what psychics had been seeing and calling the aura) so that the edges began to blur between what was known empirically and what could be demonstrated scientifically. People like Uri Geller appeared and confounded everyone by bending metal; books like *Psychic Discoveries Behind the Iron Curtain* and *The Secret Powers of Plants* started to roll back the veil between the world of sense and the world of extra-sense. Lyall Watson wrote *Supernature* and Colin Wilson wrote *The Occult.* Biofeedback techniques (and later the new science of psychoneuroimmunology) began to explore the mind and to realise that it was not the servant of the brain, as was hitherto believed; that the reverse was true and that therefore the mind, having no physical substance, may not be confined as was the brain by the boundaries imposed by the physical body and its perceptive world based on the five senses.

By the eighties the properties of superconductors had been discovered and a device called a *Super Quantum Interference Device* (SQUID) was made and used to detect the infinitesimally small fields of mental activity (areas of perception) around the head.

* *Time Magazine*, 4 March 1974.

The electromagnetic fields around the hands of healers were also examined and seen to actually change when the healer began to heal. In London a machine called a Mind Mirror was built, and the brain-wave patterns of extra-perceptive people (psychics, healers, those who could see auras) were mapped and shown to be consistent with altered states of consciousness not normally seen in day-to-day mental activity. Swamis and yogis came over from the East and allowed themselves to be tested on such machines and it was discovered that the altered states of consciousness patterns characteristic of ESP states were consistently present in them but were under a far greater degree of control than subjects tested in the U.K., due no doubt to years spent in training the mind with techniques such as meditation.

Meditation and ESP

In the same decades, a meditation movement calling itself Transcendental Meditation (TM) was growing and its leader, the Maharishi Mahesh Yogi, was demonstrating, again scientifically, that people taught to meditate did reach other (higher) states of consciousness and that everybody could learn.* This intimated that ESP was probably a lost ability of mankind which some gifted individuals, either through chance or through accident (one well-known psychic, Peter Hurkos, actually fell on his head and woke up with the gift), had managed to develop and preserve.

To be fair, the TM movement was not begun in order to teach people to develop their ESP. It was begun to teach people how to reach their inner resources, to be more in control of their thought processes, to be the architects, and not the pawns, of their own future. The inner vision which comes from practising meditation allows for a clearer view (clair-voyance?) of one's life-situation and a better deployment of one's creative energy. The TM movement was just another part of the complex jig-saw of the seventies and eighties whose patterns were beginning to join science with

* There are over 600 pieces of impeccable research demonstrating the various beneficial effects of TM.

metascience, physics with metaphysics. And creativity, man's greatest gift, with ESP states.

Readers would be entitled to ask at this point what all this has to do with consulting psychics to have your future told. In my belief it has a great deal, because firstly, a look at the progress which is being made in the recognition and mapping of these gifts puts their credibility on a firmer footing; and secondly, the understanding that such gifts are within us all removes the trappings of sensationalism and restores this kind of work to a natural, not supernatural, level. In an area punctuated by superstition and fear, an area to which people overreact violently either pro or con, there needs to be a restoration of the very objectivity which rationalists who persecute it say they admire. That done, we can proceed to look at (and deploy) ESP talents from terra firma.

Applications and Descriptions of ESP

There are many terms which are used to describe the special abilities possessed by psychics – abilities which enable them to bring us information which has an other-worldly, even extra-terrestrial quality about it. By that I do not necessarily mean anything from outer space (although some believe that the UFO phenomenon does encroach on this area) but simply not from our space as we know it, live in it and are familiar with it. However its authenticity and relevance to our life-situations are undeniable. Consulting experts who can put us in touch with such dimensions can often be a thrilling, or even spine-chilling experience, though the dimensions from which they draw their information have been described as a mere half a hair's breadth away from the dimensions in which we live and exist.

People who bring us such information may be called psychics or sensitives (general terms), clairvoyants, psychometrists, mediums, channellers, soothsayers, (gypsy) fortune-tellers, scryers or crystal-gazers, diviners or dowsers, and in a broader sense mystics, shamans, seers, sybils or prophets, plus a lot of other names not so polite, such as sorcerers, black magicians, biddies, crones – and being really derogatory (usually after a bad experience): charlatans and crooks! (As *Time Magazine* says in the same article quoted above, the psychic field has always attracted its fair share of hustlers.)

Before proceeding to classify this group of talented people and suggest how they may help you considerably to plan your life, let us distil from the above list the names and terms which you are most likely to encounter in this area now and those which may be most appropriate to the information you are seeking.

But first two more now familiar umbrella terms, coined comparatively recently by American psychic researcher J. B. Rhine: *ESP* or *extra-sensory perception*, and *PSI*, or *psychic phenomena*. The first, ESP, simply refers to the sense (which used to be called "sixth sense" and is now called the "extra sense") by which some people perceive information not normally available to the average human being (who uses but five senses: sight, hearing, touch, taste and smell). The second term, PSI, is more or less self-explanatory – it simply refers to all or any psychic occurrence or manifestation. (There is also a third modern term of which many will have heard – *PK* or *psychokinesis* – which is not an area which concerns itself with the future and hence is not in this book: it is the phenomenon by which certain gifted people, for example Uri Geller, manage to move or influence things, such as bending metal, with their minds, that is, without actually touching them.)

Contemporary ESP Descriptives

Clairvoyant is perhaps the adjectival term most commonly used today (apart from psychic) and this refers to those "who see clearly" (clair-voyance). Closely associated with this (and often these gifts overlap) are those who are *clairaudient* – those "who hear clearly". Of course both terms refer to things seen and heard which are beyond the scope of normal seeing and hearing and put their experts in touch with other dimensions.

Medium, or *channeller*, are two other fairly common terms of which most people will have heard. This area of ESP refers to those who have the ability to pass messages from other dimensions (presumably from those who have died).*

Trance-mediums and trance channellers are simply those who work in this way while in another state of consciousness, that is, in trance (Edgar Cayce, the sleeping prophet, is an example). However the information they pass comes from much the same sources as those mediums who work while fully conscious.

Sensitive (another general term) is very often used in the context of those who are aware of past circumstances, happenings and vibrations which impose themselves on places and objects (living or otherwise) and hence enable them to tell their history. Sensitives are very often used by the police when they want to track down the narrative of a crime or associate it with a person or group of persons. (Peter Hurkos was a very famous example of this and those interested can read of his exploits in helping the police to solve many crimes.)†

Psychometrist is a more specific term for sensitive and refers to the ability to tell the history of an object, and of the person owning the object, by holding it. This is a technique very commonly used today by those who consult in this area and in fact is recognized as one of the easier forms of tapping into an information source of this kind.

Diviner (or *dowser*) are not terms commonly used by those in this field although information can be passed by the means which dowsers use, which involve the use of a pendulum or divining stick to suss out information about the object of their attention. Divining techniques are more commonly used to find water and metals under the ground, to discover geopathic disturbances which may centre around areas and cause illness or disturbances, or to discover information about the health of individuals. But effectively dowsers (diviners) are drawing information from similar sources to other experts in this field and dowsing in principle can give access to information which pertains to our area of interest, for example, a

---

* It should be remembered that when this technique is used for foretelling the material passed will only be as good as the one passing it: the person "on the other side".

† Read *Psychic* by Peter Hurkos. Barker, London 1961.

very fascinating experiment was conducted on television some years ago by Ludovic Kennedy, who asked dowser Bruce MacManaway (now dead) to divine the answers to six pieces of information he had sealed in six envelopes before the programme. (MacManaway correctly dowsed five out of six answers – far above chance). But dowsing is limited in its scope in that it works on a positive/negative feedback system (the pendulum or divining stick indicates yes or no to the diviner's unspoken questions) and as such it can only be used under certain circumstances.

Crystallomancer, crystal-gazer or *scryer* denote what is perhaps one of the most misunderstood areas of perception. In fact any clear object, not only a quartz crystal, can be used by the scryer, including a bowl of water. What they are doing is thought to be projecting inner images which arise in their minds onto a surface where they can be more clearly seen: the crystal ball or the clear water. Other authorities believe (and both theories probably hold) that they are using the crystal as a focusing object, a way of helping the mind to concentrate on the matter in hand. The scryer is actually a clairvoyant using a particular technique or tool in order to facilitate the flow of information. Other psychics, though not called scryers, use similar methods to concentrate their attention, such as holding the hand of their client (though not to read the lines) or looking at a horoscope (but not analysing the aspects). It is all very mysterious and hardly surprising that strange and individualistic methods are developed by those in this field who have often had to develop their gift by trial and error. (There is one man in Spain who gives incredibly detailed and accurate health readings simply by studying the little fingernail of his client!) Suffice it to say that anything goes in this area, and one should not question the method too closely.

Seers, sybils, prophets, mystics and *soothsayers* as well as *witches, warlocks* and *magicians* are those who have studied metaphysical and esoteric teachings according to their sphere of interest and have developed or incorporated their sensitivity into this study. They are often philosophers as well, or in some way "marked" for a special task by mankind. They are people whose vocation usually sets them apart from their fellow men. They may well be partially withdrawn from the world, live in an inaccessible place, and consulting them may have to be something of a pilgrimage, much as in the ancient days the Delphic Oracle was consulted.

In the inclusion of witches, warlocks and magicians within the above category I am aware of the stirrings of unease which may be aroused in some who would view this group's activities as black or at the very least manipulative, and therefore the consulting of them to be inadvisable. This may well be true in some cases, but it is not the purpose of this book to make moral discriminations of this kind; besides which I have met many witches who are extremely helpful to their clients, as I have benefited from the profound (though maybe not the profane!) aspects of Aleister Crowley's work. Moreover I believe that the stigma attached to these categories of practitioners is as much inspired by the Church as deserved by its practitioners. (A well-known and respected magician, the late Madeline Montalban, once told me that no genuine magician worked in a black [manipulative] way because they soon discovered it boomeranged.)

The problem which seems to arise here is when religious beliefs and practices get associated with ESP gifts such as clairvoyance. It is the religious beliefs that divide people and cause dissent and suspicion rather than the ESP practices.

A classic example of this is *spiritualism*, and it may be helpful to clarify this term as well. Spiritualists have been associated with mediumship ever since it became part and parcel of the practice of their religious beliefs (in which messages are given to the congregation from those who have died). However, spiritualism itself is a religion and there are spiritualist churches all over the world (though the mediums who practise in their churches may or may not subscribe to the religious package – many are just doing a job of work).

Similarly *Wicca* is the religion of witches and in many ways it is akin to paganism, a form of devotion which was widely practised in pre-Christian times. Wicca is a religion in which psychic training is given as part and parcel of the study of *magic* (another much-misrepresented word which, according to Montalban's definition, is "a blanket word for the study of the laws of the Universe": the magician's aim being to make those laws work for him rather than to co-exist helplessly with them).

Now that some clarifying light has been thrown on a field made unnecessarily occult, it may be easier to make sense out of consulting such people, for they are truly useful and have been put on this earth with gifts that are meant to be tapped by mankind. But first, the better to understand the field in which they operate, a look at their more distant background and the evolution of their gifts.

Evolution of ESP

Before the systems of foretelling arose as we know and practise them today, divination was part of magic, which was always an aspect of man's life here on earth. Since man's earliest days there has been evidence of his deploying supernatural powers of perception: as Colin Wilson says, in his book *The Occult*, "Magic was Stone-Age science".

Evidence of ESP has also existed since time immemorial in the sub-human kingdoms and can be seen today in such phenomena as the activities of ants and bees, the homing and direction-finding instincts of eels, salmon, birds, turtles, and, in our domestic pets, cats and dogs. (Dogs can follow the scent of something totally untrackable to their owners, cats can orientate themselves and find their way home even when tied in a bag and let out in a maze.) In fact ESP, far from being supernatural, seems very natural indeed, when viewed in this way.

In ancient times, the sight and hearing of man was not what it is today and even colour-sense was undeveloped – for example Aristotle spoke of the tricoloured rainbow. At that time man used other means to hunt prey and intuit what was around the next corner – very necessary when continuity of life may have depended upon it!

Man was at that time what reductionists (ushered in by Descartes, Newton and later Darwin) may have called superstitious, which meant that he believed in powers greater than those he could see, hear, feel, taste or touch. He believed in dreams and premonitions; he not only believed in telepathy but he practised it (the "atavistic"

Australian aboriginals still do this to this day, enabling them to meet at a pre-appointed time and place deep in the outback). The world was full of unseen forces (the *huaca* of the ancient Peruvians or the *orenda* of the American Indians). Every tribe, or society, had its shaman and it was usual for them to undergo long and painful training rituals, often associated with illness, before they were considered ready for their role. (Today we know that such rituals facilitate the development of altered states of consciousness associated with ESP.)

But then came the growth of towns and with them came the need to refine and concentrate efforts, to develop interdependent skills and so gain by co-existing. Colin Wilson suggests this led to the development of the microscopic (reductionist) approach to life, responsible for the huge technological advancements of man. But with co-existence came its other face, competition, and a different kind of magic came into being – the manipulative magic of sorcerers.* Its aim was not to help and guide others but a will to control. It was the product of mankind coming together in communities and of wits being pitted against each other rather than against the hostile environment. It was probably then that the two paths of magic divided, just as, later on, astronomy and astrology became separated, to neither's advantage. As a different kind of science started to come into being, an organised, reductionist science, an organised religion started to exert its own power as well. This was hardly surprising: if man was losing touch with his own sense of the miraculous in life, of the numinous and the supernatural, then it had to be provided somewhere else.

Magic did enjoy a revival in the sixteenth century (the great age of the alchemists). But the competing trends of reductionism (science) and equally (for its own reasons) the Church, changed all that and supernatural powers were progressively frowned upon, by the former because such phenomena defied proof by scientific means as they were then deployed and by the latter because

* The difference between a sorcerer and a shaman is basically that the former practises magic in order to gain power whereas the latter does it for the good of the community.

supernatural powers, such as anything which purported to know of the future, threatened the power of the Church. Even the Bible was edited to remove the not infrequent references to supernatural powers such as clairvoyance and precognition: powers which Jesus himself undoubtedly had. Later this attitude of the Church led to active persecution of all psychics, under the declared belief that they followed the black (manipulative) path.

None the less, there were those down the centuries whose talent was too great to be repressed or whose work was initially suppressed or held to ridicule, but later brought to light. Numbered among the great through the ages who undoubtedly possessed and used their psychic powers (which modern mind-mapping has shown to be inextricably linked to creative powers) were Leonardo da Vinci, who was designing (and therefore by inference predicting the advent of) aeroplanes in the Renaissance; Paracelsus (who understood the intimate connection between mind and body which is only now being acknowledged after centuries of denial by the reductionists); Nostradamus, whose predictions have notched up confirmatory events throughout several centuries; Dr John Dee, who served as an astrologer to Queen Elizabeth I and is said to have predicted the defeat of the Spanish Armada in 1588; William Lilly, who predicted the Great Fire of London; the Comte de Saint-Germain, a sage whom Madame Blavatsky declared was one of the hidden masters of Tibet; Count Louis von Hamon (Cheiro), and of course Blavatsky herself (founder of the Theosophical Society), who had definite mediumistic powers. Coming closer to this century there was the Beast himself, Aleister Crowley, possessed of undoubted psychic powers which he equally undoubtedly misused. People such as these kept the spark of interest in these subjects alive during a long period in history when, even when not being actively discouraged, they were hardly being promoted.

Yet despite landmark names such as these – and there are many more – the emergence of the Age of Reason in the seventeenth/eighteenth centuries marked the beginning of one of the darkest periods for psychic matters, a period from which we are only just beginning to emerge. With both the Church and science actively exerting a condemnatory attitude to all things psychic, it needed a miracle. And the miracle came at the beginning of the twentieth century in the shape of quantum mechanics which, amongst other things, proved that it was possible for a body to move backwards in time – that time *was* relative. In Einstein's words (and his Theory of Relativity began the miracle), this meant that the "separation between past, present and future has the value of mere illusion". We are slowly arriving at the point where it is becoming possible to believe that anyone who has the ability to transcend time by getting information from or reaching into another dimension where time does not exist may conceivably have access to events scheduled for the future. This is precisely what those with ESP gifts have always claimed to be able to do.

Investigations into psychic phenomena were renewed in the twentieth century, with mixed results. There were accusations of credibility on the part of those conducting the research, some of which was no doubt justified. Nobody had really researched this field since the alchemists, and researchers were either inventing techniques or using ones borrowed from science which by their very reductionist nature were to prove unsatisfactory. However the scientists said they did not work because PSI did not exist and much of the early credibility of research done by pioneers such as J. B. Rhine and those associated with the British (and American) Societies for Psychical Research (founded in 1882 and 1885 respectively) was sacrificed due to questionable procedures and participants. Clearly the examining of psychic phenomena needed different procedures and it was not until the 1970s and 1980s that the gap between PSI and science began to be bridged. The result has been a tremendous burgeoning of interest, both on the professional and the popular level.

Glimmerings of How ESP Works

In the 1970s and 1980s in London, an unusual researcher began to investigate the nature of altered states of consciousness (which later came to be associated with ESP, creativity and access to a wider kind of awareness). Dr Maxwell Cade was unusual because not only were his scientific qualifications impeccable but he had also studied meditative and other mind-enhancing techniques in the East.

His original interest was in biofeedback and the remarkable results this technique was able to achieve in enabling subjects to control high blood pressure, high levels of acid in the stomach, and various other undesirable physical conditions such as the coldness of the extremities experienced by sufferers of Raynaud's disease. With the use of biofeedback instruments he taught his subjects how to relax and more importantly how to know when they were relaxed, and so doing he became aware that the altered states of consciousness which were attendant on this knowledge were giving his subjects a greater understanding and breadth of view of many other life issues. Eventually, with Geoffrey Blundell, he built a mind mirror, and with it he was better able to explore the brainwave patterns which gave indication of altered states of consciousness normally associated with relaxed awareness, a kind of diffuse feeling of well-being.

He experimented with the use of various techniques for relaxation (alert relaxation, not that associated with drowsiness or sleep) in his classes which were held in London. Students were taught Zazen and other methods of meditation and Cade also used various hypnotic techniques and music to relax his classes. His findings were published in a book written with Nona Coxhead called *The Awakened Mind* and it makes fascinating reading for those who would like to delve further. Basically Cade was discovering other ways to reach a state of consciousness which can be artificially achieved by taking mind-expanding drugs, such as LSD, at tremendous cost to general well-being. Cade called it the fifth state of consciousness (there are other states) and it is interesting to wonder whether there is any link, other than name, with Einstein's fifth (timeless) dimension.

This (fifth) state of consciousness Cade associated with manifestations of both ESP ability and creative expression. It seemed to be a state where access to a broader scope of comprehension altogether came into being. Subjects in this state often "knew" what their group was thinking or concentrating upon (in the same way that two people who are close seem to know what each other is thinking) and experiments revealed that telepathy among the group could be practised, for example, hidden objects could be found through "sending" directions to the searcher, and the content of pictures could be "thought" into the mind of a receiver. A kind of group-consciousness seemed to be in existence of a nature akin to Jung's collective unconscious: racial memories which exist beyond the scope of time.

This highly sensitive state was associated with definite brain-wave patterns, in other words it was quantifiable as being demonstrably different from normal (everyday) states of consciousness. In this state biological processes could be influenced and life-problems comprehended in their totality. Colin Wilson, in *The Occult*, likens this type of mental activity to a telescopic view of the world, quite the reverse of the reductionists' obsession with the microscopic view. He suggests, however, that the former was an essential part of man's development, in order to give him the technological know-how to function in an advanced civilisation; but now, he argues, its counterpart has to come back into the lives and consciousness of man so that he may once more become attuned to the creative side of his nature, the side that knows there is a purpose to living. ESP provides access to a different kind of knowing, the knowing that was described in Chapter 7 and in the extract from the *Time Magazine* article. Some would call it intuition: others may find this term insufficient. It is the knowing that psychics draw on; in fact one well-known psychic describes his gift as "a heightened sense of knowing", the knowing that transcends time. It is probably best described in this limerick:

> There was a young man who said though,
> I think that I know that I know,
> What I would like to see
> Is the I that knows me,
> When I know that I know that I know!

Dr Cade's observations revealed that the existence of alpha waves* (sometimes combined with theta and delta) indicated various manifestations of the fifth state. He examined the brain waves of healers and psychics and found that each activity was usually signified by a distinctive pattern. When healers began to heal their brain-wave pattern changed to indicate entry into another (fifth?) state. Likewise he observed that trance mediumship had its own very different pattern. Cade would be the first to say that this work barely scratched the surface of what he was trying to measure, but equally it provided evidence that psychic phenomena did correspond to measurable changes in consciousness, it was not just a figment of the imagination.

Then new interest was revived in another technique which had some interesting revelations to provide. Kirlian photography (invented by Russian electronics expert Semyon Kirlian as long ago as 1930) involves introducing a small amount of high-voltage, high-frequency current into a subject and recording the subsequent discharge on photographic film. The result shows an energy field, corona, or aura around the object and this energy field is seen to vary in breadth and intensity depending, among other things, on the liveliness of the object. Here was the first visible evidence of the aura psychics claimed to have been seeing down through the ages. (It is interesting to note that even early pictorial versions of the Bible often depicted Jesus with a corona, or halo around his head.)

Critics of course said that the photographs could be faked, that they did not prove anything, the usual (highly predictable!) remarks. But an expert in the field, ex-UCLA psychologist, Dr Thelma Moss (who says it clearly demonstrates the human aura), has shown

---

* Alpha rhythm is one of the basic brain rhythms, and is signified by waves between the 8 to 13 Hertz range. It is the most prominent rhythm in the whole realm of brain activity, and denotes an empty mind rather than a relaxed one. For there to be "another state of consciousness" indicated, alpha is characteristically seen with beta and theta, two other brain-wave rhythms, often in highly specific patterns. Einstein was reputed to be able to solve complex mathematical problems while remaining in the alpha state, a most unusual ability. However, Cade's research which can be read in *The Awakened Mind*, would seem to indicate that it was not an alpha-alone state.

with consecutive photographs that the coronas of healers become more intense before healing and afterwards are weaker; the same effect has been observed using the previously-mentioned SQUID to detect the field around healers' hands, and in the U.K. scientist and researcher, Harry Oldfield and his co-author, Roger Coghill*, have demonstrated through Kirlian photography the differences between the coronas (auras) of healthy and unhealthy tissue. What is fascinating about Kirlian photography is that if a leaf is cut and then photographed by these means, the field around the severed half still shows the outline of the absent part of the leaf. This *begins* to suggest that the electromagnetic field is present regardless of the physical body, which may in turn indicate the persistence of something after the physical state has gone. This and other indications of survival after death will be the subject of a later chapter.

The Nature of the Gift

Evidence is beginning to quantify ESP but there is still a long way to go. The only way we can delve deeper into the nature of the psychic gift is to turn to the empirical evidence supplied by psychics themselves, who after all have been observing and experiencing their gifts for countless generations.

Here is what one psychic, Peter Lee, has to say about this gift.

Because I am clairvoyant I am able to predict the future in many different ways. By "seeing" psychically – which is clairvoyance; "hearing" psychically – which is clairaudience; and through psychometry – divination from the vibrations of an object. I become "sensitive" with all the previous experiences of my client, which then in turn, through an intricate process of cause and effect based on natural law, enables me to see the future. I do not see the future with the human eye, but with the ever-present eye of the spirit. The spirit is beyond all human comprehension of time, human logic, space and anything that can be

* Read *The Dark Side of the Brain*, by Oldfield and Coghill. Element Books, London 1988.

comprehended in an empirical way. Clairvoyance is a paralogical art beyond the limits of logic. It is without doubt at all a parapsychology which defies the limits in which we normally see the world. The psychic expresses itself in many varying forms. Primarily and essentially it is another and more complex aspect of the subconscious and unconscious mind interacting under the wealth of information that comes from everyday experiences.

The ability to predict events on the world scene comes from reading the mind of humanity. That we have a group identity, that we are one species, is the fountainhead of how the psychic is most easily translated into the material world through receivers – commonly known as mediums or clairvoyants.*

Here then is reaffirmation of what Dr Maxwell Cade was enabling his classes to achieve – a broader (group) awareness which led to their knowing things they would not otherwise have known. Another psychic and medium, Owen Potts, whose views will be quoted more fully in the chapter on survival after death, says of ESP gifts:

I feel very strongly that everyone has the ability to develop ESP, but I think it's become obsolete. I teach development groups and I have had cases where they think they can't do that, and then suddenly they become almost 97% accurate because they train themselves to use it. I don't feel it [ESP] is necessarily a spiritual acquisition, I think it is of the psyche.

Owen Potts believes that it is the power of the client as well as the power of the psychic which enables a sitting to be successful: "One must complete the link with the client in order to pass information." Here we have substantiation of the belief that the client's attitude is all-important.

How psychics work would seem to be a matter of tuning in to the vibration of the client and although all agree that no two of them work the same way, equally do they agree that every individual has his or her own unique vibration and it is a matter of picking

* Read *The Spirit Calls* by Peter Lee. Arrow, London 1986.

this up in much the same way as the early crystal or cat's whisker radio sets tuned into the various wavebands. This is why a psychic often asks to hold an object long belonging to the client because the object has picked up the client's vibrations over the period of time that it has been worn. But not all psychics require this tuning device: Edgar Cayce, the sleeping prophet, was able to tune in on the name alone, and did not even need the querent to be present.

Another psychic, Jeanne Dixon, describes her process of tuning in (again to a vibration) in this way: "In meditating on the crystal ball, I must try to pull out of it the life of another person. This takes a great deal of strength from me, because I find that individual's colour channel and often take on his ailments before I know that I am on the right course. It is the same with tipping the fingers [another technique used by Dixon is to tip the fingers of the sitter]. That person's sorrows or physical disabilities frequently become my own, and I am depleted."

Most psychics work not just with one skill but with several. In this respect they are true channels and can channel what is needed, be it clairvoyance, healing or mediumship. This is why it does not benefit the prospective client to choose a psychic solely because of a preference for a certain type of technique: much more important to choose the person than the technique. That having been said however, it should be remembered that there are three main dividing lines between those who work in this field: those who are predominantly mediums, in that they mediate between those who have passed on and those who are living; those who are predominantly healers, who may well have other psychic gifts but prefer to work solely with healing, and those who are clairvoyant who are prepared to tell you about yourself and your future prospects.

It would be true to say that, by the very nature of the work done in this area, prediction forms a greater part of the work than with any of the other techniques. But what has been said before must be borne in mind: that the timing of such predictions may or may not be accurate.

Guides

Many have wondered about the so-called guides that psychics are said to have, some of whom, in the past, were reputed to have names that sounded more like the titles of a tall story than those of evolved discarnate souls helping their psychic brothers and sisters on earth.

Nobody quite knows what or why guides have unusual-sounding names, although there does seem to be a modern trend away from this, in much the same way as the whole field is quietening down from its previous rather sensational image.

Most psychics agree that they do have guides; some have more than one. International medium and psychic David Young has Penny, his regular guide, and Mr West, who helps him with medical problems (Mr West was a doctor when he was incarnate). Ivy Northage, who works with the College of Psychic Studies in London, has Chan. Her colleague, Elizabeth Farrel, has Nemerah. Some have put forth the theory that guides are a personalisation of the group voice, the eternal spring of advice to which we could all tap in, if only we knew how. Young's opinion seems to support this theory for he describes guides as "guiding influences", and thinks that when a composer composes music or an inventor invents something remarkable they are also guided but may not be aware of the influences around them. To me, it does not seem to matter what they are, so long as they are not used by mediums to exert power over clients through inducing the feeling that there is some kind of God speaking.

Training of a Psychic

There is usually a long period of development in front of anyone who takes up psychic work. Initially this has to do with living and suffering – going through the very trials their clients are likely to bring to them later on. There is very often a period of withdrawal from the world, or an entire life-pattern of somehow being set apart from life as most people live it. Self-knowledge is part and parcel of this journey, which is essentially at first a voyage of self-discovery. As Lee says, "if you know yourself you know others".

After this there usually comes a period of training, possibly with one person in the same field but senior, or with a group. The College of Psychic Studies in London is one of the few internationally recognised organisations that trains mediums and psychics. But many who work successfully in this field have had no formal training other than experiencing life itself and refining their gift through trial and error. Most have a very strong code of ethics, not normally voiced from the rooftops, but quickly encountered if a request goes against fundamental beliefs. Some psychics, for example, will refuse to psychometrise an object belonging to another person, feeling it to be an invasion of privacy. Others will do so if they feel the request is justified.

Most agree they need stillness in which to work, and that a client who comes in discomposed or aggressive will easily put them off. Together with an atmosphere conducive to the sensitivity of the work, they need a tool, a device for helping them to concentrate on the subject in hand. This may be inherent in their own meditative preparation before the client's arrival, or it may be an object belonging to the client. Some use the crystal ball for this purpose; one particularly talented sensitive in the U.K., David Bingham, uses a tray of sand (geomancy) and asks his querents to run their fingers through it for a few moments before he starts. Suffice it to say that all these strange and wondrous devices, which are sometimes suspected for their associations with the world of the occult, are merely looking glasses (telescopes) through which the psychic perceives other dimensions. The Tarot is also frequently used by such people.

Many psychics share beliefs in common: for example, I have yet to meet one who does not believe in reincarnation: they say they have had too much evidence of survival to believe otherwise. All (it may surprise cynics) believe in God, although their conceptions of God may vary considerably from the Christian ethic. Lee puts his views humorously: "God is not an old man in the sky."

The Chakras

Psychics are usually aware of (some can see) the chakras or energy configuration points of the body and some will tell you that the level of their psychic work varies depending on which chakra is most active during the manifestation of their psychic gift. Owen Potts teaches that the crown chakra on the top of the head is usually active in healing; that the "third eye" chakra in the centre of the forehead is active during clairvoyance; that trance mediums very often work from the solar plexus chakra and the power-to-control is always generated from the base chakra (situated near the coccyx or bottom spinal bone).

Elizabeth Farrel, who teaches at the College of Psychic Studies, says it is absolutely vital for sensitives to learn how to close down the chakras after psychic work, for self-protection purposes. Students there are taught to work only with the energy of the upper chakras, heart and above. All psychics agree that they must "close down" after working; "otherwise," says David Young, "you'd walk down the street and pick up everybody's problems."

Symbols and Sitters

One of the most prevalent questions asked by the public is why the nature of messages received through mediumship should be so trite. They feel such messages should be world-shattering, but psychics have other ideas about them. In discussing this problem, Potts had this to say: "People say why does Uncle Joe come back all the time; he never had anything to say when he was alive and he's just as banal now he's dead! Frankly, if Uncle Joe wasn't earth-shattering while he was here, he certainly is not going to be shattering over there! He is coming back, probably, to offer proof of survival, and in saying his banalities which his relatives well recognise, he's proving the continuity of his spirit."

Not all communication is done through the medium passing on conversation: some is done through the medium of the symbol.* Psychics agree that they have to become expert in the understanding of symbols, and sometimes mistakes are made in the translation of

* Explore the meaning of symbols by reading such titles as *An Illustrated Encyclopaedia of Traditional Symbols* by J. C. Cooper. Thames & Hudson, London 1978.

these into what they may mean to the sitter, or client. A symbol of the cross, for example, could be a cross to bear or a religious sign. However, on some occasions anecdotal evidence is passed to the sitter which is so startlingly pertinent as to be irrefutable. I once heard Douglas Bader describe just such an event on television. He had been a great friend of golfing commentator Henry Longhurst. When Henry died Bader happened to be opening a fête and there was a psychic working in the fête and she passed the following message through to Bader: "Your friend wishes to contact you and to tell you that the grass *is* greener on the other side." Here is an extraordinary message which Bader did not doubt came from his friend.

A few years ago I made an arrangement with an old friend and mentor in the psychic world, colour healer Ruby Thomas, to contact me when she passed over and try to get a message to me containing the word rainbow. She came through as a grandmother figure to Owen Potts shortly after her death and identified herself simply as Thomas. Like an idiot I did not expect her to use her surname (although it seems logical in retrospect because Ruby was not her real name), so I told Owen Potts that I did not have a grandmother called Thomas and he turned from her to another contact. It was only when I got home that I realised my crass stupidity: if only I had taken my own advice (suspension of disbelief) and accepted her presence I might have got a message of a lifetime. As it is, I can only offer my stupidity as an example of what *not* to do at a sitting. (Of course I will go back and try again, but I do not really believe that Spirit gives us two bites at such cherries!)

The Nature of Psychic Work

Psychic work in the main falls into the three categories mentioned above, healing, clairvoyance and mediumship. But work is done in many other ways which are worth mentioning. *Exorcism* of an unwanted spirit, or vibration or emanation around a person or place is work which can clear enormous problems. Exorcism is also done by some churches, though personally, I would prefer a psychic to do such work for me because they can communicate with the trapped soul or spirit. Then, if the site needs consecrating, by all means invite the church to do so.

Out-of-the-body experiences, including astral travel, happen sometimes to members of the public who wake suddenly from a deep sleep and the experience can be very frightening. A visit to a psychic will clarify what has happened and help you to re-centre your astral body with your physical body – though this may not always be necessary. The main thing is not to fear such experiences. People on operating tables frequently describe being out of their bodies while under anaesthetic – to my mind a good time to be out of the body!

Ghosts are discarnate souls who are somehow trapped in an area where they have had a tremendously traumatic, often emotional experience (sometimes violent death but not always). They too can sometimes be exorcised but it should be remembered that they cannot touch you or harm you.

Poltergeists and phenomena which result in vases appearing to fly across the room and smashing, etc, usually occur around a pubescent child in the family. The turbulent emotions released at that time in life have somehow found an extraordinary outlet. Often the child is psychic but the gift is suppressed. Bringing a psychic into the home or taking the child for blessing and healing may help.

Hypnotism is not per se part and parcel of the psychic profile but it is a technique which releases innate psychic powers and as such needs to be performed under highly qualified supervision. Some hypnotists are regressionists: they will regress a subject back into a past life. It is not a technique for beginners to play with; in a sense it is an artificial way of reaching innate ESP and other powers within us. Hypnotism can have great value but in general its purpose should be for other than psychic work.

One final (general) term should perhaps be clarified as it seems to inspire dread and unnecessary fear: a *seance* is simply a medium-conducted meeting of people wishing to communicate with discarnate souls. In joining together they give more psychic power for the spirits to draw on in order to make their presence felt. (The sitter's power is always drawn on for this purpose, even in an ordinary, one-to-one session with a medium. It is nothing to fear, since the power drawn upon is namely the power of the emotions, hopefully of love.)

The Negative Face of the Psychic World

Far too much importance is placed on the evil side of psychic work. It is generated largely from fear of the unknown or from religious groups. David Bingham has something interesting to say about any group who would exclude and annihilate others: he thinks they are into power because a truly evolved attitude to life is a "live and let live" attitude, a "judge not lest ye be judged" attitude. Bingham has noted that when exclusive groups exist in the psychic world it is often a sign that they wish their views to be the only views acceptable.

However, Peter Lee is in no doubt that there is an evil or negative face (akin to the Christian's hell) in the spiritual plane. In his book *The Spirit Calls* he writes: "There *is* a definite force for evil ... there are spirit forms that tempt." In another part of the book he says: "I am convinced that below the earth plane in which we live, on a psychic and different material reality (due to its vibrational rate) there is a totally negative plane."

Owen Potts does not agree. He thinks we are all a mixture of good and bad, otherwise we would not be here. "I think we're a bit of everything. I don't feel from the word go that there is anything that comes from the power of spirits that's evil: I think the same power is utilized in the mind to turn it into good or evil. Many years ago I looked into witchcraft, I looked into voodoo and all those sorts of things just to see what they were, and honestly I must say I found it was all in the mind ... I did not find anywhere that there was a power of evil coming from the spiritual elements."

I leave you with these two points of view and the observation that at some stage in our lives, in order to grow, we will probably attract to ourselves what is the innermost and darkest aspect of our own nature. Psychologists call it projection and see it all the time in our relationships with those who mirror these aspects of our psyches. I think there is another type of projection which enables the

attraction to ourselves of psychic essences which are not helpful.*
Sometimes these can eventuate from playing with a ouija board.
Ouija boards are not in themselves evil but if we are in an open and
manipulative state when operating them something can happen
which is not in our best interests. One must always protect oneself
from external influences when working in this field, which is why,
in the main, it is much better to consult those already working in
this field than to attempt to dabble in it unwittingly. A teacher or
class is always advised for the beginner. As Bingham says: "If you
were wanting to be an electrician, you wouldn't start by putting
your hand into the fuse box."

Critics of the Psychic World

The psychic world has always had more than its fair share of critics.
These usually fall into three main categories: religious groups
(the Church); scientific groups (the Establishment); and, perhaps
surprisingly, a third group, magicians. And it is this last-mentioned
group which comprises by far the most damaging and destructive
critical element, because in many ways they are achieving the same
effects as psychics, but with very different methods.

The term magician, when used in this modern sense, bears little
or no relation to the magic which has been the subject of discussion
in earlier parts of this chapter. We are referring now to conjurors,
people with gifts of sleight-of-hand; people whose profession depends on deception. It is those people who present psychics with
criticism that is the hardest to counter, because in many instances
they can duplicate psychic phenomena (PSI), though by known
(deceptive) means, involving sleight-of-hand, misdirected attention, and patented paraphernalia.

Because of the skills they have developed in this respect, they
say they are better able to spot frauds than scientists, and they seem
ever eager to do so (which in itself is interesting, because psychics
in return are perfectly happy to co-exist with magicians). Somehow

---

* Some experts working in this field believe that possession is responsible for
some cases of madness; cf. the work of Edith Fiore and William Baldwin in the
U.S.A.

the magicians feel threatened by psychics, though not the other way round.

One world-famous American magician, James Randi, spends, it would seem, as much of his energy in attempts to expose psychics as he does pursuing his own career. Randi has directed his interests towards many psychics over the years, and has claimed to repeat many if not all of their phenomena.

In an effort to expose one Russian psychic, Rosa Kuleshova (the subject of intensive scientific investigation in Russia because she claimed to be able to "read" with her fingertips), Randi allowed himself to be blindfolded with pizza dough, a mask and a hood, and then proceeded to drive a car in traffic. He then claimed that his truly remarkable feat "was pure deception, just like hers". However he refused to tell investigators how he had done the trick, simply avowing it was not by psychic means. It seems to me that until he proves that he did not do it by psychic means he is just as big a suspect for fraud as Kuleshova may well be in reverse!

More recently, the editor of the prestigious U.K. science magazine *Nature* used James Randi in an attempt to expose a French scientist, Beneviste,* who claimed to have scientifically demonstrated for the first time the principles of homeopathy. Homeopaths work with incredibly dilute solutions or remedies, so dilute that not even one molecule of the substance from which the remedy was made exists in the solution. Yet they have been demonstrated empirically over many centuries of homeopathic practice to have potency in respect to curing illness. Beneviste carefully repeated his experiments over a five-year period, and asked several other labs in various parts of the world to independently repeat them for him as well (he knew they would be controversial when published). The results were confirmed by all labs. Yet when Randi was taken to Beneviste's lab, and Beneviste was asked to repeat the experiment in his presence, he managed to throw it into complete disarray.

This in itself is interesting, adding further fuel to the contention, supported by quantum theory, that the observer *does* influence the

---

* Two articles appeared about this controversy in *Nature* magazine during 1988, namely 30 June and 28 July.

result (especially, one imagines, if those producing the result are extremely sensitive to atmospheres or working with extreme dilutions of solutions). It also indicates that Randi may well have some powers of one kind or another (even if it is only the power of his reputation, the power of his presence).

To my mind, nothing is proved or disproved by the endeavours of those who probably work in a manner which may even be (though it probably is not) half a hair's breadth away from the manner in which psychics work. That Randi has succeeded in throwing Uri Geller into similar disarray on a TV programme set up for the purpose does not necessarily prove Geller a fraud; but even if it did, how is it then presumed to prove as frauds every single psychic who ever worked? Psychics who work, as does Geller, in the public eye, are not always those with the greatest professional probity – which is not meant to be a reflection on Geller.

It seems to me that this argument will keep on being waged until scientists discover satisfactory methods to examine psychics which do not resort to employing the chicanery of others to expose what they believe to be the chicanery of psychics.

Health and Psychic Consultation

I have left this area until last but it is by no means the least reason why you should consider consulting a psychic. Often psychics can provide invaluable insight into the cause of an illness, or even suggest an alternative line of enquiry. For the fact remains that people who consult psychics regarding illnesses are usually those whom the doctors have not been able to cure, and therefore alternative lines of investigation may be the only ones not tried. The psychic will not conduct the treatment and they are always careful to refer only to those qualified to do so. Sometimes the psychic will suggest a line of enquiry which the patient can ask the doctor to follow: many have been helped in this way, that is, by psychics uncovering unsuspected illnesses which may underlie a known (diagnosed) illness. This function is quite separate from the healing function, when there is thought to be an exchange of energy between the healer and the sufferer – a recharging of their batteries.

Much is known of the healing aspect of psychic work but very little is known of its potential for diagnosing and delving into the causes of illness. Psychics such as David Young believe that if the cause of an illness is known (and it may lie many years before the illness's onset) then a starting point for a curative course can be ascertained.

As a young journalist, I organised a very interesting experiment with David Young to test his diagnostic ability. The results were published in *Woman's Own* in the early 1970s* and went far beyond my expectations. One of the leading naturopathic clinics of the day agreed to my suggestion that I should present six cases with medically attested histories to Young, one after the other, my only stipulation being that there were to be no visible signs of their illness and that they should all be wearing similar clothing, that is, towelling robes.

Young correctly diagnosed each illness, often giving much detail surrounding the cause of the illness. In one instance he actually itemised the three things that were worrying the patient, the three facets of his illness of which he had complained when he was admitted.

But the real test came from a completely unplanned aspect of the experiment. Unbeknown to me (or anyone involved) the clinic's director had decided to acid-test Young's abilities by introducing as a "red herring" one of their own nurses as a "patient". However, equally unbeknown to the director of the clinic, this nurse had a medical history of her own which Young proceeded to itemise in intimate detail, even to the Indian name she had been given when nursing with the nuns of a nursing order in India.

On several occasions during this test Young would approach a patient and whisper something to them. This was his own personal psychic "code of ethics" at work: he refused to divulge certain intimate information without first getting the permission of the patient. In the case of the nurse he whispered in this way to her and was subsequently told by her that he could tell her employer

* The articles referred to appeared in *Woman's Own* on 18, 25 August and 2 September 1973.

what he did not know: that she was a suspected early multiple sclerosis sufferer. This in effect constituted the "double blind" factor in the experiment, the ultimate requirement of scientific technique, that nothing was known of this by either the experimenter or the experimentees. Of course it has not been replicated, which is another requirement of this technique.

Later, when I came to work in another field that interests me, the field of health, I discovered other gifted people who could diagnose, as could Edgar Cayce, at a distance from their subjects, and yet still provide invaluable insight into the physical (and psychological) conditions of their enquirers.

Psychics and the Aura

It is my belief that diagnosis from the subtle energy fields of the body, such as the aura, may ultimately replace or certainly reduce any need for those illnesses ever to manifest on the physical level, because evasive action can then be taken before the illness ever occurs. The work of Kathleen Kalina in America (who is a self-styled medical psychic and a leader in her field) and in fact gifted psychics all over the world could be put to the test in this respect. Another leading American psychic, Joseph Ostrom, who specialises in aura readings, and who is the author of a book on the subject,* also believes that there is a place for psychics in medicine, as there always has been in healing.

Psychics such as Ostrom have observed that every individual has his or her own unique colour ray, composed of several colours fundamental to their expression in life. (Jeanne Dixon talks of getting "on-line" with the colours of an individual under study, and one well-known dowser in the U.K., Wing-Commander Clive Beadon, also experiences this phenomenon when he "dowses" for people.)

The aura has always been known to contain many colours, and Owen Potts, who works a great deal in the field of health, has said that the colours in the aura "are a direct reflection of the state of

* Read *You and Your Aura* by Joseph Ostrom, published by Thorson 1987.

the health of the individual under study". The popular phrase, "seeing a person in their true colours" comes to mind, making one wonder how much we have forgotten that our language still reflects.

Many years ago, in St Thomas's Hospital in London, a Dr Kilner built a screen whereby ordinary (that is, non-psychic) people could view the aura, because in his belief the diagnostic value had importance. Work like this often begins in an obscure setting which is either discredited or forgotten, to be resurrected many years later when the rest of the world has caught up with the advanced thinker who started the study.*

Dowsing and Radionics

Readers may be familiar with the radionics movement, which acknowledges the special gifts which dowsing has in this area. Dowsing is another way in which the intuitive faculty is harnessed for the good of mankind, and many dowsers can work with a lock of hair or a drop of blood to produce a full report of the subject under study. Homeopathic remedies or colour therapy may then be prescribed. It is certainly an avenue worth investigating if one is suffering from the effects of a difficult-to-diagnose complaint. Dowsers are also invaluable for checking houses and in particular sleeping quarters for electromagnetic pollution and geopathic stress. The earth, too, has its own aura, and more and more it is being affected by what is being done to it in the name of progress.

In Conclusion

This chapter has been a long one because the psychic field is probably the single most important (and complex) area in which knowledge extraneous to the range of our normal perceptions can be brought to bear on our options in this life. It is impossible to give too many directions about how to use this area, because it depends on what experts may be at your disposal in your area.

---

* Health aspects of ESP will be covered in more detail in my future book, *Life Forces*.

However, we live in critical times and it is hoped that whatever insights may have been given will encourage those who cannot see for themselves to find somebody good who can help. It may take several tries to get a good result (knowledge of this kind is never easily won) but persistence will be repaid.

There is another reason why everybody should visit a psychic or medium at least once – and that is to take the opportunity to collect personal evidence of the reality of this field. Once a person has gathered subjective evidence and experience of this nature, never again is the existence of other dimensions doubted.

Booklist

Any book by or about a well-known psychic, e.g. Edgar Cayce, Doris Collins, Jeanne Dixon, Peter Hurkos, Peter Lee, Lobsang Rampa, Doris Stokes, etc. Any book by Rudolph Steiner.

Cade, M. and Coxhead, N. *The Awakened Mind*. Wildwood House, London 1979.

Fortune, D. Any book but they are not recommended for beginners.

Hurkos, P. *Psychic: the story of Peter Hurkos*. Barker, London 1962.

Jung, C. G. *Man and his Symbols*. Aldus Books, London 1964. Picador, London 1986.

Montgomery, R. *A Gift of Prophecy: The phenomenal Jeanne Dixon*. Bantam Books, N.Y. 1966.

Roberts, Jane. *The Seth Material*. Prentice Hall, N.Y. 1970.

Ostrander, S. and Schroeder, L. *Psychic Discoveries Behind the Iron Curtain*. Bantam Books, N.Y. 1973.

Ostrom, Joseph. For title see footnote page 92 and also (on the aura) Beesley, R. P. *The Robe of Many Colours*, published by the College of Psycho-therapeutics 1968.

Sugrue, T. *There is a River*. Henry Holt, N.Y. 1942.

Watson, L. *Supernature*. Hodder & Stoughton, London 1973.

Wickes, F. *The Inner World of Choice*. Coventure, London 1977.

Wilson, C. *The Occult*. Hodder & Stoughton, London 1971. Mayflower 1973.

9
ASTROLOGY
Its Diverse Untapped Potential

We are born at a given moment, in a given place and, like vintage years of wine, we have the qualities of the year and of the season in which we are born. Astrology does not lay claim to anything more.
C. G. Jung

Astrology is the most holistic of all foretelling arts in that it allows for interpretation on any level to which the astrologer can aspire. It gives scope for both the thinking and the intuitive functions, and a gifted astrologer may also use ESP. Yet it has a discipline, a structure, which, if adhered to, will yield results even for beginners.

As such it is often the initial technique chosen, especially if an exact birth time is known. But even if it is not, there is much valuable information to be gleaned from having your horoscope cast, ranging from the help it will give you in understanding your character and potential (knowing your strengths and weaknesses, both physical and mental, inherent and inherited), to comprehending the way in which you may be drawn to, and relate to, others, and the possible pitfalls you may encounter in so doing. It can show you the grand plan of your life (though not the intimate detail) and thus help you to make the best possible use of that plan.

With this sort of structure, the earlier its facilities can be incorporated into your life, the better. All other consultations you subsequently select may merely serve to illuminate and more sharply delineate trends which have been identified within the framework of your horoscope. Furthermore, this one umbrella of knowledge known as astrology incorporates many subsidiary spokes, or techniques, which can and should be applied to your life at appropriate times. They are all discussed in turn in this chapter.

Background

Astrology has been around for thousands of years. Nobody knows its exact place of origin, but there is evidence that it was practised by the Chinese, the Hindus, the Aztecs and the Egyptians – people who lived thousands of miles from each other, separated by mountains, deserts, forests and seas. One authority claims the Chinese practised it in 1752 BC: another actually says it was well-established in China in 2637 BC. In India, where very few records have been preserved, it was known to flourish in 1500 BC, although how many centuries earlier it is difficult to say. There is some evidence to indicate that horoscopes were drawn up there in 3102 BC.

The high priests of the Mayas were also said to have observed the heavens 4,000 years ago and the Mayan calendar was said to be able to distinguish (without duplication) any given day in 370,000 years! The Maya link is an interesting one and some historians think that Hindu and Chinese explorers may have travelled overland to the Behring Strait, then across to Alaska, and down the West Coast to Central America. (Anthropologists have shown that there is an uncanny resemblance between Hindu and Mayan culture and religious rites.)

Astrology certainly flourished in ancient Egypt, Chaldea, Phoenicia, Babylon and was also practised by the Hebrews. The art spread to Greece and Rome, and the Arabs are thought to have carried it into Spain and France and ultimately it was introduced through various sources to Britain.

Suffice it to say that wherever there was an ancient civilisation a form of astrology was practised and its prevalence may have arisen as a natural consequence of star-watching, for the principles of astrology would seem to come from this source. It is thought that over many hundreds of years of observations (maybe even thousands), ancients and wise persons noticed a correspondence between the positions of the planets and the types of personalities born. However, their initial interest was understandably in events, since it was one of the few ways they had of anticipating what might be about to befall them. The moon's movements were of tremendous importance in those days and many of the original systems of astrology were based on the lunar cycle.

It does not seem to have mattered what local system astrology was based on, be it the sun, the moon, or, as is still the case in the East, the stars; the general conclusions and body of knowledge are surprisingly similar. None the less there is one school of astrological thought which believes that astrology was not so much based on the observation of, and correlation between, the movements of the heavenly bodies and life-patterns here on earth, as on an increasingly complex system of symbolism – which could explain its links now with psychology. Probably it owes a little to both ancient symbolism and planetary correlation.

It seems to me, however, that the base of reference is really quite irrelevant. Regardless of whether you have your chart calculated by ancient Eastern or modern Western methods there will be striking similarities in what is said. All the rivers of astrology flow from the same source, and what seems most important in this day and age is to find a good practitioner rather than insist that he/she follows a particular discipline, be that Western or Eastern. That having been said, it should also be noted that as a general rule, the system of astrology which has developed in an area is usually most appropriate for those born there.*

Evidence to Support Astrology

Arguments wage back and forth as to whether the tenets of astrology can be supported or not, and it is not really the purpose of a book such as this to go into them, because it is presumed that anyone who is envisaging using astrology in their lives is going to test it in the only way that really matters – by using it. But readers may well

---

* The origins of astrology are a fascination, and have great bearing on the type of astrology which is practised in any given area; for example, Chinese horoscopes are based on the year of birth rather than the day, because birth-days are rarely recorded there. However, the history and background of astrology, apart from its origins, has been well documented and because it is not enshrouded in mystery and misconception, as is the history and background of techniques using ESP, its more recent documentation has not been attempted here.

live with people who like to argue about its principles, and so I am offering a few pointers (indications) as to where research backs up astrological principles.

Possibly the best source of supportive information comes from the work of French statistician and scientist Michel Gauquelin (see booklist on p.115) who originally tested astrology in order to debunk it. After analysing the birth-charts of people in similar professions and finding in each instance a definite correlation between the type of profession chosen and the position of certain key planets in their horoscopes, he began to change his mind, albeit slowly! Now he has also indicated by similar means that children do inherit bits of their parents' horoscopes: in other words his findings indicate that astrology *is* faithful to heredity in this way. (Critics used to say that the astrological chart, being based on the birth time, could not possibly take into consideration inherited traits, which are known to be passed on from generation to generation. Not only has it been shown that they do, but it has also been shown that when birth times are interfered with by artificially inducing the birth, a popular habit with obstetricians today, it interferes with the child's horoscope, seeming to destroy some of the links with parents' horoscopes ... Could this interfere with relating? I think it does and so do many other astrologers.)

I would recommend the reading of any of Gauquelin's books to those who would like to follow the process whereby he put astrology on the statisticians' map.

There was also some interesting research done in America some couple of decades ago by the scientist Frank Brown. Brown took oysters away from their natural habitat (where they were accustomed to opening their shells at high tide to feed) and placed them in a laboratory 1610 km inland in a different time zone altogether. Over a two-week period Brown observed that the oysters adjusted the time to open their shells to when the tide *would* have been high in their new site. He realised that they must have made the adjustment according to the moon's phase, because there was no high tide or any other tide anywhere near them! In other words they revealed extreme sensitivity to the moon's rays.

It has been known empirically for years that the moon does affect those of us who seem to be particularly sensitive (terms like luna-tic and moony come to mind!). So is it not therefore as likely that we are in some way affected by each and every planet, even though we have not yet found a way of measuring how? Researchers in Germany, following this principle, did a study which showed that there were four times as many car accidents during a period of high sun-spot activity. Other researchers have shown the effects of Saturn and Mars on iron filings in a laboratory.

To my mind, none of this matters, since the proof of the astrological pudding is surely in the eating – which is the point Sir Isaac Newton made to the astronomer Halley, when the latter criticised his interest in astrology: "Sir, I have studied it, you have not," Newton replied. However research such as Gauquelin's has proved invaluable in forming a bridge between the Establishment and astrology, and anything that does that has to be good. We owe a great deal to Michel Gauquelin and his wife Françoise, who helped him in his original research.

Sun-Sign or Media Astrology – Its Other Face

If there is one type of astrology which has familiarised the general public with the subject it is sun-sign astrology, as it is written in the newspaper and magazine columns and sometimes broadcast or televised: daily, weekly, or monthly predictions for the twelve sun-signs. Publicity has proved to be a double-edged sword for astrology in this respect, for whilst this type of column has familiar-ised people with astrology and taught them many home-truths about themselves, the system of prediction used by media astrologers has had to be simplified to the detriment of the subject. This is not to suggest that some media astrologers (Patric Walker comes to mind) are anything but fine practitioners, but they are working with one hand tied behind their backs.* It is a tribute to astrology that despite

* While reading this part of the book, a fellow astrologer suggested a richer analogy: "both legs shackled and blinkers on to boot."

this disability it still manages to show enough of its true colours to have won many followers by these means.

Sun-sign astrology is in fact based on the *month* of birth and is interpreted through the twelve sun-sign, or personality types. Any predictions thus made are therefore relevant to one-twelfth of the population at any given time. To expect accuracy from this basis is preposterous. True astrology is based not only on the *month* of birth, but also the year, the day and the time of birth, all of which is connected to the place of birth – giving four more factors or variables which together refine the view of the birth through a very precise lens. Precision is something sun-sign astrology can never achieve.

To serious astrologers, one's sun-sign, whilst being quite an important factor in the judging of one's horoscope, is none the less only one of many factors which contribute to such an assessment. In fact the information given in this way can be misleading unless its relationship with other factors in the horoscope is taken into account; it is the position of the sun in relation to all other planets in the horoscope which gives it its special flavour.

So (for example) whilst you may have your sun in Aries (in common with one-twelfth of the population) and have an Aries-type personality in that you are forthright, enterprising, courageous and inclined to leap before you look, all these traits can and will be modified or accentuated by the relationship your sun makes with other planets in your horoscope. Thus the Aries traits which you display, whilst showing marked similarities with those of other Aries people you know, will not manifest themselves in exactly the same way or indeed at the same time. The variables are so great as to provide each and every individual who is born with the sun in Aries with a horoscope that is truly unique.

Even identical twins have differences in their horoscopes. The passing of a mere four minutes of time leads to a different degree being recorded on the ascendant, or rising sign, it being another extremely important factor in a horoscope. It is also by no means uncommon to find twins born with their moons in different signs and this can have a differentiating effect on character too.

Applications of Astrology

A horoscope or natal chart is a fundamental tool for mapping your future. Thus everybody should have his or her horoscope cast at some time or other in their lives – preferably at birth, because material about the individual who has been born is then available to the parents from day one of the life. Not only does it then provide a valuable blueprint of the child's nature and requirements before it can speak and communicate those needs, but also it enables the parents to make informed plans about the child's future. For example, many parents put their child's name down for a school on the day they are born. How much better a choice they could make if they knew in advance what sort of education would best draw out and develop their child's unique talents.

There is no escaping the fact that a horoscope does provide the key to both character and potential. It also says a lot about the likely preferences and interests of the individual under scrutiny. It has been said that a horoscope is like a roadmap of the life ahead. That is a good analogy if it is borne in mind that a roadmap contains a selection of many routes, any one of which the map-reader may choose to follow. But it does act as a guide to the general area and this is precisely what a horoscope or natal chart can do – and no more. Furthermore, it is the single most important piece of information available about an individual and as such it was long the custom in the East (where astrology has never been thrown into disrepute as it has in the West) that when a new family member arrived, the horoscope was prepared as a matter of course.

Preparing Your Own Data for Horoscope Purposes

To have your horoscope cast, three vital pieces of information are required and they are the time, date and place of your birth. Birth times provide by far the greatest area of challenge in your quest for accuracy and you should question all relatives closely who may recall anything about your birth. (See introductory remarks in Chapter 2.)

For future parents it is possibly important to know that if you intend recording your child's birth times, then the moment of the first breath (or cry) is considered to be the one to record.

Even if your birth time has been recorded on your birth certificate (as is the custom in the U.K. more recently) it is as well to question it (especially if it appears to have been "rounded" to the nearest quarter of an hour – busy hospital staff can and do get side-tracked). Some astrologers will attempt to refine and rectify an approximate birth time (see next section) but so long as your time is reasonably exact, say to half an hour, it will give a fairly accurate result.

The use of noon (a practice still followed by some astrologers when a birth time is not known) should never be agreed to. It leads to a completely wrong ascendant or rising sign being given to the subject of the horoscope. (Watch out for this when ordering computerised horoscopes.) When the birth time is not known and cannot be discovered it is better to try a rectification technique. But if that fails and produces a non-conclusive result, the degree or position of the sun in the horoscope should be placed on, and used as, the ascendant.* This is because, apart from the ascendant, the sun is the most important factor in a horoscope and co-inciding it with the ascendant, while over-emphasising this, at least eliminates the false importance of the "noon" ascendant.

Rectification of Birth Times

If you do not know your time of birth and cannot discover it, an astrologer can attempt a rectification process, working back through the milestones of your life in an effort to see a pattern, a co-incidence of happenings, upon a particular degree of the zodiac, which can then be used to ascertain the birth time. Thus the more accurately the times are recorded of your life's milestones (moves of home, marriage, divorce, births of children, etc and including the DOB of all those with whom you have had major relationships) the more likely the technique is to prove effective.

---

* This is called a sunrise chart, for the time of the birth is taken as the time at which the sun rises.

Rectification is an extremely difficult and laborious task and not many astrologers will attempt it. However there are specialists who will and their work is highly paid and much sought after. At the end of the day, however, you will never know for sure what your birth time (and therefore ascendant) is – which is why so many astrologers, myself included, favour co-inciding the sun with the ascendant if the pattern of your relationships does not confirm an alternative line of study.

Erection of Your Horoscope by Computer

Computers have transformed astrology, but many people do not realise that they have not taken over the interpretation side, only the calculation side. The prevalence of computers has led to the availability of computerised horoscope calculations which can provide, at a reasonable price, all the planetary positions necessary for the calculation of your horoscope. However this, like the incidence of sun-sign astrology, is a two-edged sword. To have your horoscope calculated by computer makes eminent sense: the data is good for all time and the computer is not likely to make a silly arithmetical mistake as is the overworked astrologer. However, to then accept the computerised interpretation (or reading) of your data in the form of a character reading with future predictions is usually as invidious as believing all that you read in the sun-sign astrology columns. That said, it is only fair to say there are good computerised horoscope interpretations on the market, but they are usually written by astrologers with national or international reputations, because computerised readings are only as good as the person who writes the data base, that is, who has fed the words into the computer. Therefore you are charged to be pretty selective about whose computer horoscope you choose and to remember that it will never replace a personal reading by an astrologer because no computer can ever synthesise all the variables in your chart.

Erection of Your Horoscope by Experts

If you have not yet had your horoscope cast by a reputable astrologer, the sooner you do so, the better. It provides the structured accompaniment to any other information you may receive by other means. It is the jumping-off point, and will give enough food for thought to keep you busy for several years!

Once you have had your horoscope erected or calculated, you can then ask the astrologer to do an annual update for you, and do what is known as a year's predictions. Some people ask the astrologer to look ahead for a longer period of time than a year, but I believe this diversifies the astrologer's attention and also predisposes clients into a living-in-the-future mode. To know the general trends for the year ahead is usually quite sufficient to make adequate plans. (Besides, most astrologers will pin-point anything of importance which they feel you should be aware of ahead of the year in question.)

Thus going to an astrologer could and probably should be an annual event, timed, if possible, to coincide with your birthday which is when *your* year ahead begins. Some families give this as a birthday present.

Consultation Advice

Many people do not realise why regular visits to an astrologer are beneficial. At the first visit the natal chart, containing information about character and potential, is usually considered. This in itself can take up an entire reading of several hours' duration. After that it is your progressions and predictions for the year in question that are concentrated upon, plus any aspects of your character which the astrologer thinks may be relevant to comment upon considering what lies ahead. For example, if a relationship seems likely in the current year, the astrologer may suggest looking at the way in which you are likely to relate to others on close terms, with a view to avoiding pitfalls. Thus the information in a natal chart is always relevant as growth or experience constellate it in the life pattern, giving rise to the expression of some traits which may hitherto have been dormant.

A visit to an astrologer should be of at least an hour and a half's duration. There is so much ground to cover and you would be advised to jot down beforehand what directions you particularly want the astrologer to take because there is enough information in the chart to keep you both there all night!

Arranging the Consultation

Much of this has been covered in Part 1, but a few things need to be mentioned which have particular relevance to astrology. The first of these is that many astrologers have a hobby horse in the study, or a favourite line of approach. Whilst you should be prepared to listen to what it may tell them about you, there is a limit to what any one technique or direction will produce. You need to work with an astrologer who is happy to use several techniques, such as judging the compatibility between yourself and another person (which requires them to erect and compare both horoscopes) using horary charts where necessary (in order to judge the outcome of an event) or using harmonics to study a close relationship. Such techniques further refine basic astrology and enable special insights to be gained about specific situations. However astrology is not designed to provide specific details in the main: it will tell you when the time is ripe for a key relationship in your life, for example, but it will not tell you whether he or she is tall, dark and good-looking! That is the domain of psychics which is why the two techniques are often complementary. With the exception of horary astrology – a technique which can produce details in the hands of an expert – you would be wise to distrust an astrologer who gives you details such as those in the example above, or, if they turn out to be accurate, suspect them of being psychic as well. Astrologers are trying to clean up their act and divorce it from the more indefinite results achieved by psychic means of prediction. This is not to suggest astrologers decry psychics: they just want the boundaries between the two techniques better understood by the general public so that the latter do not expect things of astrology which it cannot deliver.

Your relationship with your astrologer is going to be highly personal and its success will depend on how well you get on together. What suits your friend may not suit you, so try to have a conversation with the astrologer before you book an appointment – ask them how they work – ask them what sign they are if you like!

Bear in mind that it is not possible to wander into an astrologer (as you would a psychic) and expect them to give you a reading off the top of their head. True astrology necessitates work of some hours before the client appears, which is why it can never be cheap if it is done properly.

However, once your astrologer has calculated your natal chart, it will be on record for all time, and then you can expect faster results if you want to discuss something. And just as the astrologer will take notes of each session you have, so in effect should you, because it will be a way of judging the accuracy of what you have been told.

Questions

A seer once told me that if you are ready to ask the question, you are ready to receive the answer – which may seem obvious but in effect there is a lot more in that remark than is first realised. Astrologers will not tell you everything about your chart at the first meeting. Some matters will not have "ripened" at that point. However you are entitled to question them and the deeper your line of questioning, the more likely you are to extract from them a few home truths which they had been putting off telling you about yourself!

Questions which may produce highly relevant answers (not always the ones uppermost in your mind) are those which seek to understand the patterns in your life: situations or relationships you tend to get into more than once. Try some of the following lines of enquiry:

Why do you think this pattern is continually recurring in my life?

Why is this person behaving in this way?

Given my particular nature and abilities, how can I improve my relationships/finances/career prospects/health/quality of life, etc?

Of the things you have told me which are outlined as beneficial, are there any steps I can take which will improve these prospects further?

Of those which may bring problems, which am I likely to have to confront and which may I be able to avoid?

What effect may the past have had on me and my relationships with brothers, sisters, teachers, employers, etc? (Your astrologer may need to do more charts to throw light on some of these complex issues for you.)

You can see that for the first time in your life (possibly) you will be able to probe deeply into your nature and its subconscious motivations. Hopefully you will also see how vital it is for you to choose your consultant carefully; preferably somebody with psychological training or with counselling training, although most astrologers are natural counsellors by the very nature of their work.

Understanding the Language

Astrologers, because they love their subject and the tools with which they work, may frequently, during your reading, refer to the planets and call them by name. They may make remarks like: "Venus is square Mars in your chart and that is why you find harmony in relationships difficult to achieve."

It is important for you to understand that it is just their way of speaking – that the planets are not beaming things at you. Leading American astrologer Zipporah Dobyns once expressed the opinion that she felt much of the criticism which was levelled at astrology by religious and other groups was because of the way astrology was often presented as if the planets were running the world and everybody in it. This is not the case and astrologers are well aware of this. Nevertheless some of them do tend to speak in those terms.

At those times it is vital to stop consultants and ask exactly what they mean. Probably they are reflecting upon an aspect in your character and its correlation with an aspect between the planets in your horoscope. Equally, it is important to realise that the planets do not cause events or problems in your life; they merely reflect the condition of it or a set of circumstances – circumstances which can usually be controlled: that is why you sought your consultation in the first place.

Astrology is one of the consultative techniques which does benefit from a telephone follow-up when you can ask all the questions which arose in reviewing your reading. Make an appointment to do so as soon after your consultation as possible, otherwise the astrologer will forget the details of your chart.

Expectations versus Results

Astrology's facility is to be found in providing a ground-plan of your life, not, as it has been stressed, in providing you with intimate detail and colour. Astrology can tell what main areas of your life are likely to be highlighted at any given time but there is even likely to be some ambiguity about those: for example, the areas of career, status or public image, aims and attainments, parents, or parent-figures (such as employers) all come under the same house or specific area of attention in astrology! Sometimes the skill of the astrologer can refine that area down, sometimes not. So astrological technique is very much of a dialogue between consultant and client, after which some very useful deductions about future moves and attitudes can be made. One of the chief stresses on astrology in the past has been the demand for it to perform in a way in which it is not ideally designed, that is, primarily as a vehicle for predicting the future, but what outlines astrology does give in this respect are likely to be very well-structured time-wise.

Divisions of Astrology

The fundamental tool of astrology is the natal chart, but there are many other techniques for extracting knowledge in given situations in life, about which many people are totally unaware. The following are descriptions of the most important techniques (including the natal chart) and what can be derived from them.

Natal chart readings otherwise known as *horoscopes* or *birth-charts*. Information about career, love relationships, health and finance can be derived from this at any time. Sometimes the directions will be clearer than others. However if more information about a certain area of life is required, harmonic charts can be set up, which are derived from the original horoscope and are known to throw better light on a particular area of life. Indian astrology has made use of many of these techniques for thousands of years.

Synastry techniques, including *composite charts*. For anyone thinking of settling into a steady relationship, these are highly recommended. In this technique the two charts are examined side by side (synastry) or combined (composite) to ascertain what of relevance a couple may need to know about each other. This kind of technique is invaluable for detecting possible trouble-areas in a relationship (areas where they are less likely to understand each other) and thus help avoid the head-on conflicts which are so damaging.

Horary astrology. This valuable technique for judging an event or situation is undergoing a revival and horary astrologers say they can judge anything from the location of a missing pet (or missing piece of jewellery) to the outcome (and ramifications of) an important meeting. It is important to understand that it is not the horoscope of a person, but a horoscope erected to answer a question. For that reason the question has to be carefully formed and the time at which the question was asked meticulously recorded.

Mundane astrology is about politics, governments and countries, and is only of personal use in the consideration of a move or protracted trip abroad. An off-shoot of it which concerns itself with elections is called electional (that is, political) astrology.

Astro*Carto*Graphy is another vital weapon of modern astrology. It was devised by American Jim Lewis (who calls it Astro*Carto*graphy) as a "means of identifying locations at which an individual might experience certain parts of his or her potential". Apparently there are parts of the world which nurture certain aspects of our nature better than others. Obviously this technique has uses both in deciding where is a good place to live and also in examining why certain places seem to be "unlucky".

Rectification. This has already been discussed as a technique for discovering the degree of the ascendant when the birth time is unknown. The degree of the ascendant is important since it fixes the timing in a chart (which can never be judged accurately without it). Also the ascendant gives a great deal of information about how the person will appear to others. It is worth recording here that psychics and mediums can often get information about birth times from a relative who is dead, so that is an avenue worth pursuing. Two people I know were helped in this way: one with an exact time which had been given through more than one medium, another with an approximate time – "early hours of the morning".

Harmonics. Harmonic astrology was revived by the late John Addey, although he would have been the first to say that its principles have been known and practised in India for centuries. The technique used by harmonic astrology is that of dividing the horoscope circle of 360 degrees by a given number (known as a harmonic) and then to reposition the birth planets according to the dictates of this division. Division of the horoscope circle by certain harmonics is known to bring to the surface matters relating to a particular area of life (numerology rears its head here), for example, the Indians use the division of nine (Navamsa) to look at the marriage prospects.

Some harmonics indicate health conditions or tendencies to them. Addey did a study of nonagenarians by this method, and found that certain harmonics were significant among them.

Anyone who understands wave formations will be fascinated by the concept of harmonic astrology – possibly one of the better analogies is to imagine that you are tuning in to a particular radio station on a particular frequency in order to receive a certain type of information.

Techniques like this can be non-holistic, however, if there is a tendency to become obsessed with a part to the exclusion of the whole. This is why the warning was issued about astrologers with hobby horses.

Children's astrology and vocational guidance. These are not areas of study which require special techniques for setting up charts, but they are getting special mention because they are areas which tend to be overlooked. Astrology lends itself brilliantly to the giving of insights into young people, provided such insights are not pronounced as if existing on tablets of stone. Astrologer Zip Dobyns says she sees a lot of harm done by astrologers making pronouncements about children and whilst I consider her comment important enough to record here, the fault does not lie with the system but with its users.

The parent-child relationship is an extremely formative one on both sides if it is allowed the flexibility to develop as needed – and the needs of each child may vary. Parents tend not to see their children as the adults they will become and this is understandable, for children tend in the main to mirror only those parts of their natures which their parents like to see. Of course they have lapses but if they are firmly sat upon they will become rarer and rarer, until adolescence that is, when the whole unruly spectrum will announce itself!

Yet belief-systems, from which parenting is structured, do not have to be altered to allow scope for individual expression; the only factor which may need varying is the method by which they are applied, and information of this nature is available in the natal chart of the child.

I will never forget the moment I first erected my son's horoscope. He was in the terrible 'teens and we were having battle after battle. Suddenly I saw him as an individual; an individual who was like this and not like that, who could be approached successfully by some means but not by others . . .

I changed my approach to him (thought not my general belief-structures) overnight. For example, I started explaining my reasons for taking certain attitudes with him, something I had never done before. (He was an Air Sign, and they like to know the reasons for things.) There were many deeper insights than this simple one I have described, including insights into myself. This had such a profound effect on me that I wrote a book called *Astrology and Your Child* and I believe that this is an area of astrology which will be increasingly used – hopefully not abused.

Vocational guidance is the logical progression of this area of astrology and much can be gleaned about innate gifts and interests.

Career decisions are having to be made earlier and earlier in the educational picture, and there would be fewer square pegs in round holes if astrologers were consulted. A good career guidance astrologer will take into consideration the child's personality needs as well as the contingencies of earning a living, etc. For example, whatever the child's literary talents may be, there is no point in choosing a career as a novelist if the child *needs* company. Novel-writing is a lonely profession.

Chinese (Eastern) Astrology

The Chinese astrological system is based on a twelve-year cycle* whereas our system is based on a twelve-month cycle. This system (Rat, Ox, etc) is winning increasing popularity in the West and is sometimes used as a complementary system to our own. Experimentally, it does appear to work, as anyone who has read the descriptions of the particular birth year-type will agree. However, purists say that this system, like our own, works best when the birth time is taken into consideration as well as the year. One of the best books ever to have been published on the subject is by Theodora Lau, *The Handbook of Chinese Horoscopes*, and I refer readers to it. Much rubbish has been published about Chinese astrology, chiefly by Western astrologers.

Transpersonal Astrology

With the growth of psychology which has occurred in this century, there has been a corresponding movement to explore the very real talents astrology has to offer in regard to psychological insights as

---

* The Chinese horoscope cycle is not really twelve years as many people believe (in contrast with the Western system of twelve months). In fact a complete cycle takes sixty years and is made up of five simple cycles of twelve years each (Rat, Ox, Tiger, etc). Each cycle is calculated from the second new moon after the winter solstice. On 2 February 1984 the seventy-eighth recorded cycle began – the Chinese lunar calendar is the longest chronological record in history, dating from 2637 BC when the Emperor Huang Ti introduced the first cycle of the Chinese zodiac.

gleaned from the natal chart. It has been said that this is in effect a map of the psyche; whether this is simplistic or not is still the subject of debate. However there is little doubt that an interpretation of the psychic energies as represented by the planets in the horoscope and the aspects which they make to each other, does give a very clear picture of the psychological make-up of the person under study. It will show where the individual is likely to come under stress in the expression of a trait or aspect of the psyche, and where there may be ease of expression. It will indicate both the outer personality, the persona, the cloak that is assumed to face the world, and the inner self. (What is thought not to be shown on the chart is the soul.)

Most modern astrologers study psychology these days, partly because the nature of astrology lends itself so well to this study, and partly because of the work they do with people. Leading astrologer and founder of the School of Transpersonal Astrology in Britain, Dr Liz Greene, has said that an astrologer who does not incorporate psychology into his or her training and advisory work in malpractising. There is little doubt that this is one of the major movements of this century as far as astrology goes, and many of us who see astrology at work in this way believe that it provides analysts and psychotherapists with a short cut to the understanding of the psychological complexes of our fellow human beings that will do away with hours spent on the analysis couch or in counselling. This is not to suggest that work of this nature should not proceed at the pace suited to each client, but simply that the understanding of any underlying psychological pressures is seen so much more easily and speedily through the astrological lens. This is not the appropriate place to go deeply into this subject, but merely to present the technique and its availability, and to suggest that it will prove helpful to anyone having emotional or relationship problems. However, consultations of this kind should not necessarily be considered as a single visit, but rather as an ongoing experience of the deep, underlying currents as revealed in the natal chart. Part 3 will provide addresses of how to get in touch with astrological counsellors of this nature.

There are other categories of astrology which I have not

mentioned. Those interested in exploring more can find out about them by contacting the Urania Trust in London, whose address appears in Part 3.

Overview

Astrology deserves its popularity. We live in the space-time continuum of earth and astrology is one way in which we can understand these dimensions, to learn how to live and move within them to the best advantage. There will always be those who argue that studying the movements of the planets cannot possibly help or affect us, but they have missed the point: in order to see the pattern we must look away from ourselves to something which will give us our bearings in the scheme of things. We have to synchronise the watches of our lives by looking away from the microcosm to the macrocosm.

Booklist

Popular books for introductory purposes: anything by Evangeline Adams.

Collings, J. *Astrology and Your Child.* Granada, London 1980.

Goodavage, J. *Astrology, The Space Age Science.* New American Library, N.Y. 1967.

Goodman, L. *Sun Signs.* Pan, London 1968.

Greene, L. *Star Signs for Lovers.* Arrow, London 1980.

Lewi, G. *Astrology for the Millions* (1962) and *Heaven Knows What* (1985). Llewellyn Publications, U.S.A.

Introduction for students

Any book by Margaret Hone but in particular *The Modern Textbook of Astrology.* L. N. Fowler, London 1951.

Jones, M. E. *The Guide to Horoscopic Interpretation.* David McKay, N.Y. 1974.

Mann, Tad. *The Round Art.* Dragon's World, U.K. 1979.

Mayo, J. *Teach Yourself Astrology.* English Universities Press 1964 and *How to Cast a Natal Chart.* L. N. Fowler, London 1967.

Omarr, S. *My World of Astrology*. Fleet Publishing Co., N.Y. 1965.
Parker, D. and J. *The New Compleat Astrologer*. Mitchell Beazley, London 1984.

More advanced educational reading

Addey, J. *Harmonics in Astrology*. L. N. Fowler, London 1976.
Carter, C. *Astrological Aspects*. L. N. Fowler, London 1960.
Davison, R. C. *The Technique of Prediction* L. N. Fowler, London 1971.
Ebertin, Reinhold. *The Combination of Stellar Influences* (translated from the German). Ebertin-Verlag, Germany 1940.
Gauquelin, M. *Cosmic Influences on Human Behaviour*. Futura, London 1974 (and any other Gauquelin titles).
Any book by Alan Leo.
Luce, R de. *The Complete Method of Prediction*. N.Y.
Robson, V. *Astrology and the Human Sex Life*. W. Foulsham, London 1963.
Sepharial. *The Manual of Astrology*. W. Foulsham, London 1962.

Horary astrology

Lilly, W. *Christian Astrology*. Regulus, U.K. 1985 (reprint of seventeenth-century text).
Watters, B. H. *Horary Astrology: the Judgement of Events*. Valhalla 1973.

Mundane astrology

Baigent, Campion and Harvey. *Mundane Astrology*. Aquarian Press, London 1984.
Carter, C. E. O. *An Introduction to Political Astrology*. L. N. Fowler, London 1951.

Chinese astrology

Lau, T. *The Handbook of Chinese Horoscopes*. Arrow, London 1981.
And there are many more notable books not mentioned.

10
PALMISTRY
The Palm: Storehouse of Information

Palmistry is a study worthy of the attention of an elevated and inquiring mind. Alexander the Great

Of all the techniques for interpreting the future, palmistry requires the greatest amount of personal contact between client and consultant. Awareness of this is all-important to those who like to keep at least a desk between themselves and their consultant! However most really good professional palmists do not work directly from the hand all the time: they take handprints, so that they can keep records – but first they like to observe the hand, its colour, shape, etc.

Possibly palmistry is one of the best known of all foretelling arts and also the least understood. "And the gypsy read my hand" is a remark which has echoed down the ages, giving rise to a number of misconceptions, of which more later.

Because palmists work with a living pattern, something in the here and now, it is a very good medium for judging current states of mind and health. If we project the frequently-used analogy that the horoscope is like a seed, a blue-print of the person-to-be, then the hand is the living plant or tree that grew from the seed – the result of the adaptions of that unit of life over the years to environmental, interpersonal and other pressures. Because of the complementary view by astrology and palmistry, I like to work with them both (and with graphology, which gives another view again) because I am fully aware, to continue the analogy of the seed, that if it falls on stony ground it will not develop its full potential, as will the seed falling on fertile ground, the only sure way to judge that outcome is to look at a pattern existing in the here and now – the hand or the handwriting.

Palmistry should always be considered as a technique if there is a problem in the here and now, for example, why am I feeling so low ... or why can't I complete this task ... or what are all those new little lines which have appeared on my fingertips? Palmistry not only embodies the facility to inform you where you are now (which incidentally implies there is a very accurate map of time on the hand, and there is) but also to provide a detailed record of what has just passed, as well as indications of what may come to pass. The hand could be said to be the living manifestation of the present, which in turn is the result of the sum total of decisions taken in the past, and as such will indicate directions for the future, in much the same way that a stream originates in the mountains, finds its direction on the plains, and ultimately flows into the sea.

Many people think that we cannot change our future, but the lines on the hand confirm that we can. For those lines can, and do, change with changes in attitude and resultant action. To witness this is one of the great joys of reading a palm, because it confirms that we do have free-will – although we might do better to think of it as willpower. More than any other pattern, the palm shows that character is destiny: the stronger and wiser we become, the stronger is the path of our destiny.

Background

Palmistry is such an ancient art that nobody really knows when or where it started. One school of thought believes that it was first practised by Chinese savants as early as 3200 BC and that during the next few thousand years it spread westward through India and Persia, finally reaching Europe where many Greek philosophers (including Pythagoras and Aristotle) studied it avidly. (For example Aristotle tutored Alexander the Great in palmistry.)

An alternative school of thought suggests that palmistry's origins were in India, and Indian expertise in the art, which persists to this day, lends favour to this argument. Certainly it was known that the Hindus studied a science known as *Samudrika*, involving the contours of the body and the shape of the limbs, from which they gained a knowledge of mentality and character. It is thought that

Hastarika, or the study of the lines on the hand, developed from that.

It is also thought that much of this early knowledge was lost when manuscripts and works on all the branches of the occult were destroyed during one of the Mongolian invasions of India. At that time Hindu palmists scattered; some were said to have sought sanctuary in Persia, while others wandered as far afield as Egypt and Greece (here we pick up the threads of the alternative legend). We know for sure that there are records of Hindus, Chinese, Japanese and Persians having carvings of the hand and its mysterious palmar lines in their sacred monuments and temples. It was believed, certainly by the Hindus, that palmistry and astrology were parallel subjects and used to be taught together as being indispensable to each other. However, somewhere along the line (except perhaps with the Hindus) palmistry lost even more credibility than astrology and from that time, certainly in the West, palmistry and those who practised it were looked at askance.

Nevertheless, in unabridged and less modern versions of the Bible there are definite references to the hand as a medium for seeing into the future. An example occurs in Job 38:7 which reads: "God caused signs or seals in the hands of all the sons of men, that the sons of men might know their works." A further reference in Proverbs 3:6 speaks of "the length of the life in the right [hand] and in the left wealth and honour". Accepting that parts of Proverbs were written fairly late, supposedly under Hellenic influences, we have the tie-up with the written records which were known to have been kept in such sources as the *Codex Erlangensis* from as early as 1100 BC.

Hopefully this potted history will go some way towards redressing palmistry's shrouded past, giving it a few roots of respectability in accordance with its sister study of astrology. However, it is still being attacked by such organisations as the Church, along with astrology, where the concept that man has any kind of right to knowledge about his destiny is still anathema. Knowledge of course is power, and even the most credulous can draw their own conclusions about what may be the real reasons (not the given reasons) for such a stand.

The Palm and Predicting the Future

How much of the future does the palm display? In the hands of somebody as gifted as Indian palmist Mir Bashir it could be thought that pretty well everything is there from birth to death. But small events in the life are not normally seen; it is the sum total of them that is seen. As Sasha Fenton says in *The Fortune Teller's Workbook*: "There are just too many years on any hand for the smaller events in an enquirer's life to show up. If every little happening were to be displayed, the hands would have to be the size of grand pianos!" She argues that the general or overall outlines are there, together with potentials and possibilities.

Sasha's comments raise other fascinating aspects of palmistry, aspects which fundamentally divide palmistry into two schools of expertise: the gypsy school (cheiromancy) and the analytical school (cheirology), and her remarks have prompted me to explain the differences between these, as they lead to more misconceptions about palmistry than anything else.

Cheiromancy

Among the earliest practitioners of palmistry in Europe were the gypsies. Most authorities believe that they originally came from North India and were descendants of the Jats. Certainly their language is sprinkled with Indian words and this link could explain their tremendous expertise in reading palms. They tend not to do so in the same way as the Indians do now, however, although even in India there is some blending of the two basic techniques and it is hard to discern where one technique begins and the other ends.

Cheiromancy, although it takes into consideration the lines, marks and prints of the hand, is far from being derived from the detailed measuring of the same which occurs in cheirology, which is the more scientific (deductive) way of reading hands. Cheiromancy definitely employs a psychic faculty, and the hand can almost be thought of as a tool for tuning in to the vibrations of the person under study. Unfortunately this has led people to believe that almost anything can be told from a study of the hand, whereas what is more true is that the hand has always been an excellent focus for psychic observation.

Cheirology

Cheirology incorporates two other studies and has in part originated from them: cheirognomy, the study of the shape of the hand, and dermatoglyphics, the study of the ridge and furrow patterns found on the palm. (Police work is almost entirely devoted to dermatoglyphics, that is, the study of fingerprints.) Cheirognomy takes into account not only the shape of the palm – whether it looks squarish or rounded or elongated – but also the relative length and breadth of the fingers and thumb, fingertip formation, flexibility and the shape of the joints, colour and texture of the nails and skin, plus the way the hands are used in gesture. Famous palmist the late Beryl Hutchinson said that the observation of shape (cheirognomy) is the ABC of hand interpretation, and a never-failing source of interest, whether in television talks, newspaper photographs, or in ordinary contact with our fellows. A good cheirognomist will always note your gestures and also where you habitually wear your rings. Nothing is sacred – or secret!

A good cheirologist, while working exclusively with measurements and observations as does a scientist, will none the less use the same kind of diagnostic skill which singles out the good family doctor from the mediocre one. Nowadays we would be more likely to call this faculty intuition (Faculty X), in this case reflecting the ability to come to the correct conclusion about a bewildering plethora of data. In summation the difference between cheiromancy and cheirology could be said, simplistically, to be that the one (cheiromancy) is intuition guided by knowledge and the other (cheirology) is knowledge guided by intuition.

The Consultation

When you consult a cheirologist (a consultation will take an hour or two) they will first take prints with fingerprint ink. This enables them to see clearly the minor markings which are not otherwise so visible, also to take comparative measurements and to draw a time-scale around the life-line and several other lines.

In order to establish a base-year on the life-line, the palmist may need to ask you several questions, such as "were you ill in 1960 or 61?" Many people view this as a leading question but it is nothing of the kind – the palmist simply needs to know an accurate date in order to be able to pinpoint other dates accurately.

Most palmists use a magnifying glass to study the hand, and you will see why when you observe the minute patterns which they are trying to decipher for your benefit. A millimetre scale is needed to mark off years in the life-line, so you can fully realise why they need to be absolutely sure of the timing of one major event in your life, before attempting to proceed with other years and other events.

Everybody knows that no two sets of fingerprints are alike in the world, not even between identical twins, and the same is true of the ridge patterns on the palm. These integral parts of the skin's patterning never change, and Indian tradition sees these as the sacred key to man's karma; karma being a much-misunderstood word which simply means "for every action there is a corresponding reaction".

The lines, and their formation, plus their tendency to change and develop, are thought to be the indication of the free-will factor in the hand: certainly the palmist looks to the lines of the left hand for information about inherited traits and to the right for insight into what we may have done with those traits.

Once the palmist has assessed what the hand has to convey, your consultation can take very much the same form as a consultation with an astrologer. As with the astrological chart there is such a wealth of information available that some kind of direction or concentration of attention is essential. Since it is likely that you will have made the appointment because of a situation arising in your life, that should be expressed and take precedence, but it is always wise to let the palmist give a general reading first, because clients with problems often fail to see the wood for the trees. What ensues here should give you some idea of the tremendous scope of information available from the hand.

Health in the Hand

The importance of the hand as an indicator of health, both mental and physical (as if the two can be divorced) cannot be underestimated. It is the belief of many professional palmists, including myself, that medical students will eventually learn about the palm as a valuable adjunct to diagnosis, and early diagnosis at that. Perhaps prophetically, an article in the *Journal of the American Medical Association* in 1954 said much the same: "Despite widespread and sometimes unnecessary use of numerous laboratory tests in the day-to-day clinical practice, diagnostic methods that require no special apparatus and that depend only on simple observation can play an effective role in obtaining clinical information about patients. In this connection, the human hand is a unique organ from which an extraordinary amount of clinical information may be derived."*

At this time in medical history, tremendous break-throughs are being made in the understanding of diseases and their origins, and one of the major advances in this respect has been in the realisation that ill-health, as manifested in gross physical disease, is the *ultimate* sign of a breakdown, not the initial one – the signs were there long before the disease appeared.

What is also being recognised is that the causes of ill-health are coming directly from the result of excess of stressful input into the brain, input which is in turn funnelled down the spinal cord to settle in the body's weakest link.

The hand is known to have more nerves than any other part of the body (there are thought to be 2,600 nerves in the hand, compared to only eight to the square inch in the leg) and it is posited that because of this the hand is an accurate recorder of the traffic of thoughts (in fact that is what the whole of palmistry is based on). In the hand there are areas corresponding to every organ in the body, which, incidentally, are also found in the feet. (Reflexology or zone therapy is structured upon this concept and it is known that the massaging of the zones in the feet which

* This extract appears in Dr Eugene Scheimann's book, *A Doctor's Guide to Better Health Through Palmistry*, listed below.

correspond to sluggish or diseased organs in the body can often improve the condition.) What is less widely known is that the same is also true of the hand, but the hand, being so intimately linked to our mental expression, does not lend itself so readily to relaxation therapy as do the feet and hence the latter are more customarily used. However, there is no denying that on the hand there is a map not only of our character and destiny but also of the state of our physical body: the hand, as a living entity, reflects the state of that living entity.

There have been several theories posited as to why the hand should have such a close link with the brain: Professor Wood Jones, previously Professor of Anatomy at Manchester University and author of *The Principles of Anatomy as Seen in the Hand*, has offered the suggestion that the area of the brain which corresponds to the hand is larger by far than that which is linked to arm, facial, trunk and leg movements.

Professor Wood Jones also observes that "in the human brain the large hand area is situated immediately adjacent to the older area in which sensation and movements of the face are represented." If this is the case then it is exactly this area which is attracting the attention of scientists studying the link between the mind and the body and its effect on the brain, so although there is much work yet to be done, it would seem that the hand is closely connected with our state of being. Beryl Hutchinson noted that calm people have fewer lines than those who are highly strung, in particular the paucity of lines on the hands of certain African tribesmen known for their ability to endure pain and even injury with relatively little shock. She discovered – as have many palmists interested in health – that a multiplicity of lines and even changes in the skin-ridge patterns take place when people are unwell or sickening.

It was Noel Jaquin, author of *Health in the Hand*, who discovered or rediscovered for the West the fact that although skin-ridge patterns are part of the unchanging panorama of the hand (something the criminal profession is well aware of – even when fingerprints are burned off they grow back), their structure does deteriorate when certain diseases are present: upon recovery the condition reverses. Jaquin observed that with such break-downs, or clouding of the basic ridges of the skin of the hand, each has its own insignia linked to certain diseases. Arthritis, for example, can often be detected early by the appearance of a veiling of mostly fine, upright lines on the percussion side of the hand (just under the little finger beneath the main transverse line) and cancer is sometimes signified by a more general breakdown in the pattern. Another pioneer in this field, Dr Charlotte Woolf, whose research mostly concentrated on psychiatric conditions, confirmed this – as does Mir Bashir, who says that cancer is always to be expected when there is a general breakdown in the skin ridge patterns. Bashir says he often refers his clients to a doctor if he observes such signs – seeing, as he does, 1,500 clients a year for the past forty years he has had too much experience not to act upon what he sees.

Fevers and glandular disorders and disturbances in the endocrine system sometimes confer upon the palm a granular appearance. (Amateurs are advised not to try and assess these signs for themselves, as there are other causes for them.) The life-line itself (the line around the ball of the thumb) when islanded and broken, is also an indication of periods of disturbance in the flow of the life-force or body energy. However, a short life-line or even a broken life-line is not of itself an indication of a short life, as many people fear. Rather it is an indication of the way the life-energy flows in that individual, and when or where illness or other stress has caused the flow to be interrupted.

It is impossible to mention all the research indications of health in the hand here: that could occupy an entire book. Suffice it to say that when there are either physically-based or psychologically-based disturbances, the hand will afford early signs of them, not only in the appearance of the palmar surface, but also in the way the hands are moved. For example, there is a particular type of severe psychological disturbance which is signified by a total absence of hand-swinging during walking. Our gestures, as well as our palms, speak a very special language to those who can decipher it.

Love and Marriage

One of the best uses to which a consultation with a palmist may be put is in the understanding and resolution of love relationships.

When a love object enters the life, sanity leaves it. People who consider themselves to be quite well-balanced can become completely disoriented when they meet somebody "special". Worse, this fever is often complicated by another fever, and that is the overwhelming desire for a relationship, so that the love-object becomes tinged with a potential for the future which may be far beyond its suitability.

In this respect a visit to a palmist can be invaluable, because not only can the palmist indicate the relative importance of the current love-relationship, but also give some kind of an idea about the future and its potential for further relationships.

There is a tendency, especially among young women, to put up with disturbing traits in the love-object, traits which are beginning to alarm them on one level, which they suppress either because they do not feel they deserve better, or because they feel this may be their last chance to satisfy their very natural cravings for having a home and family.

Everything has its season, including love, and signs of major relationships are usually indicated on the hand. This in itself is comforting to know if one appears to be in an emotional desert. And even if the hand reveals the future to be uncertain in this respect, steps can be taken, attitudes can be changed.

Compatibility and the Hand

A consultation at this time can be useful for another purpose – assessing compatibility, getting to know what sort of person might be suitable for a long-term relationship. The unconscious side of the nature, which is often the side which unwittingly attracts the opposite sex, is visible on the hand, hence traits which might otherwise be projected on to another, causing dependency at a deep level, can be recognised and the process begun to bring them into consciousness.

A compatibility study of both hands will show attitudes to many issues which may potentially be sources of dissent with a long-term relationship but which do not show up at the start. Material values, long-term sex drives, attitudes to love (idealistic or realistic), readiness to raise children, all are issues which can be judged on the hand. It is amazing what can be worked out between a couple if it is known and confronted from the outset. Many consultants are familiar with remarks such as this from married clients: "I understand that trait now and make allowances for it, but when we were younger it caused terrible fights and accusations, some of which are hard to forget." True, there is no substitute for experience in life, it is the best teacher: but does it always have to be your own experience?

Children

The desire for children and the importance they may assume in your life is shown on the hand more reliably than actual births. However there are palmists who have a very good record with judging births and also the possible sex of the future child, and they do so from the so-called affection lines which cut the palm horizontally at the side just under the little finger. Lines arising vertically from them are said to be boys, whereas lines at an angle are said to be girls. Sometimes the birth of a child shows as a line arising from the life-line. Such little lines are often called lines of creative effort, and one or two of them at the appropriate time of life could certainly indicate a birth – however their judging, as with all indications in the hand, is a complex matter, depending on more than one indication.

There are one or two clear indications known to palmistry which indicate that giving birth may be a difficult or lengthy process. This is one area in which awareness can reap tremendous rewards because provision can then be made for the birth to occur in supportive surroundings.

Career and the Hand

The hand is better for judging vocational skills rather than for assessing actual professional choices. It certainly indicates where talents and interests may lie from an early age and as such can be of extreme value in advising the young.

It is also useful in later life as well. Sometimes a person has had to suppress a talent or ability because of the pressures of education, or because of the contingencies of earning a living, and this suppression can be so complete as to have totally eradicated the awareness of the talent. The hand can indicate such areas, and hobbies can be chosen so that creative outlets are not blocked for ever. Suppression does not help the flow of life-energy.

Commerce

A business hand is very distinctive, as is a hand which recognises the value of money. The message on the hand is always fundamental – what one *needs* to fulfil life rather than what one *wants*. If a person has a need for a substantial income in order to feel fulfilled, it is important for him or her to recognize this fact, so often overlooked in vocational guidance. A business hand is often an earthy hand (which does not imply lack of intelligence), yet the person is often directed into professions which do not fulfil the need to have property, possessions and a solid base.

Palmistry Overview

As a technique for discovering your future potential, palmistry is hard to beat, but the problem of finding a proficient practitioner is more acute in this profession than in any other. Those who are visiting the East for any reason should always try to have their hands read there, for palmistry has ever been promoted and perpetuated there and even simple street palmists are often very good. In the West it might be advisable to discover where a good palmist lives and make a decision to visit when you are able. There are more cheiromancers around than cheirologists, and these also can be very good, but it is as well to realise that it is not true palmistry. One of the greatest palmists alive today, Mir Bashir, who was born and learned his palmistry in Pakistan and India, has said, in comparing the two methods of hand-reading: "You can't completely trust a sixth sense: you have to have technical things. You must be able to repeat the process of interpretation over and over again from the text book. That's what palmistry is about: not just once, but every time. Like medicine – a diagnosis."

Bashir, who has seen over 50,000 clients in a lifetime of consultative palmistry, believes that it is a calling, a calling which clearly indicates itself on the hand of the future palmist with several significant signs. In 1946, the year before Bashir left India to come to London, he made a pilgrimage to a certain temple in Madras of which he had heard. There in a book thousands of years old he was shown an ancient prediction which referred directly to him stating the exact date, time and place of his future birth, and what his profession would be – that of a palmist.

Predictions such as that make one wonder whether we know anything at all about the art of foretelling in this day and age.

Booklist

Bashir, M. *How to Read Hands* (Thorsons) and *The Art of Hand Analysis.* Muller, London 1975, 1981.

Benham, W. *The Laws of Scientific Palmistry.* Knickerbocker Press, N.Y. 1900 and *How To Choose Vocations From the Hands.* G. P. Putnam, London 1935.

Cheiro (Count Louis von Hamon). Anything he has written but specifically *Language of the Hand*, Jenkins, London 1968, and *Book of Fate and Fortune*, Arrow, London 1985.

Fenton, Sasha, *The Fortune Teller's Workbook.* Aquarian Press, Wellingborough 1988.

Gettings, F. *The Hand and the Horoscope.* Triune Books, London 1973, and *Palmistry Made Easy*, Wiltshire Book Co 1966.

Hutchinson, B. B. *Your Life in Your Hands.* Paperback Library Inc, N.Y. 1967.

Jaquin, N. Any publication but especially *The Hand Speaks*, Lyndoe

& Fisher, 1942; *The Signature of Time*, Faber, London 1950; *The Human Hand, The Living Symbol*, Rockcliff, 1956; *The Hand of Man*, Faber, London 1934.

Saint-Germain, Comte de. *The Practice of Palmistry*. Newcastle Publishing Co Inc 1943.

Scheimann, Dr E. *A Doctor's Guide to Better Health Through Palmistry*. Parker Publishing Co, N.Y. 1969.

Spier, J. *The Hands of Children, and Hands of the Mentally Diseased*, Routledge & Kegan Paul, London 1955.

St Hill, Mrs C. A. Any book.

Wolff, Dr C. *Studies in Hand Reading* (translated from the German, 1936); *The Human Hand, The Hand in Psychological Diagnosis, A Psychology of Gesture* (the last published by Methuen, London 1951).

11
GRAPHOLOGY
Handwriting: The Graphic Giveaway

Spoken words are symbols of mental experience. Written words are symbols of spoken words. Just as men do not have the same speech sounds, neither do they have the same writing. Aristotle

Over the years, graphology has become one of the most widely accepted forms of divination. It is in fact a science, a social science, and as such depends on research and observation, not ESP. However, a good graphologist always uses intuition, as does a good doctor, a good psychologist, etc.

Graphology is based on the indisputable fact that no two people in the world write the same, just as no two people in the world have the same fingerprints, the same voices, or the same physical appearance. Handwriting is considered to be an externalised sign of our individualism, and as such it is arguably a blue-print of what comprises that individualism. It is a personal symbol of who we are, and just as a symbol contains a subject in its entirety, so a sample of handwriting reveals all the ingredients of the psyche of the individual under study.

Why is this so? It is easy to see why a palm may be a map of the person to whom it belongs, because it is part and parcel of him, but handwriting is surely contaminated by a combination of the times and customs into which we are born, the language in which we have learned to write, the way in which we are taught to write and with what, plus how we feel at any given moment when we decide to put pen to paper. How can each sample of writing we produce be a living symbol of everything we contain, everything we ever were or may be? Because, simplistically (and to quote one of my finest teachers, Peter Marshall), "handwriting is brainwriting". Handwriting is a sequential symphony of the smallest, most controlled, most elegant gestures we ever make with our hands, that is, writing, and gestures of any kind are a self-revealing language. They give our game away because the hand that makes them is governed by the central nervous system which in turn is governed by the brain. But just as the process of writing is partly unconscious, so does handwriting contain elements of both the conscious and unconscious mind – the psyche as a whole. This premise is supported (though not proved) by the observation that like psychology, graphology has never been able to discover a criterion of difference between the male and female brains and the way they write. (Sex cannot be ascertained by handwriting; both "masculine" and "feminine" elements are present.) However, it is known that in each of us there are tendencies of the opposite sex, and the fact that these are usually part of the unconscious side of our natures suggests that handwriting, in revealing such traits, is produced by both conscious and unconscious elements of the mind: mind in its entirety. Certainly handwriting is something which requires our entire attention – try watching the television while writing a letter, or talking to someone!

Not only the contents of the mind but the state of the mind are revealed in handwriting, which is why there are slight changes from day to day, mood to mood. But the basic form and shape of the letters hardly varies – it is minor factors only like size, slope and pressure which change slightly to reveal mood. (When spirits sag, for example, our posture and gestures often do likewise, and part of those minute changes of gesture are conveyed through the flagging hand into the handwriting.)

Small wonder that handwriting electrifies us all and on some level we are all graphologists. We recognise the handwriting of friends without having to read their signatures because unconsciously we have made an assessment of the characteristics of that writing. Indeed, handwriting has been traditionally recognised as being unmistakable for years – signatures have honoured receipts, payments of goods and money and legal documents since time immemorial: forgery is a crime. In other words society acknowledges an individual's handwriting as a unique feature.

Doodles

Even a casual doodle is known to reveal much about its architect, and many psychologists use them as valuable adjuncts to understanding their clients' complexes. In the United Nations a decade or more ago, it was noticed that waste paper bins were being emptied at unnaturally short intervals: spies had cottoned on to the fact that certain political leaders (Khrushchev was one) were giving the game away, if not in what they were saying, in what they were doodling!

But how is it that handwriting cuts across the trappings of alphabet, education, style, custom, etc? Whilst it is true that these things do leave their mark on handwriting, just as the fashions of the day leave their mark on dressing, it is a superficial mark, a mark put there in much the same way as a corset shaped an Edwardian lady. Underneath the essential handwriting, underneath the Edwardian corset, is the natural form which does not change. One test of this is to try writing with your other hand or with your foot in the sand. The way you form the letters is essentially the same – the hand, foot, etc are merely instruments for the dictates of the individual mind.

A fascinating offshoot of this was witnessed when subjects were hypnotised and told they were first Napoleon, then a forger, then a child, etc, and were asked to write something whilst each role was being hypnotically assumed. The hypnotised subjects' writing did change dramatically to reveal traits commonly associated in handwriting with the personality structure of each of these decisive roles – but it was the subject's subjective view of that role that was recorded, revealing despotic traits, for example, in respect to Napoleonic writing, but not actually reproducing Napoleon's handwriting. More than anything else this interesting experiment probably indicates the limitless potential we all have within us. Was it not Goethe who said that every trait that had been witnessed in man he could find in himself?

The Page as a Self-Portrait

Probably it is worth including in this preparatory discourse the theory laid down by Max Pulver, author of one of the all-time classic graphological works *Le Symbolisme de l'Ecriture*. Pulver suggested that handwriting was an exercise in form and space. The empty page waiting to be filled was symbolic of the writer's mind and of his own position in the dimensions of space and time – his world – spiritual, social, material, etc. Pulver thought that all were not only mirrored in his handwriting but in the position (stance) he took on the page. For example the left, where the writer begins, represents the past (mother, roots, origins) and exactly where he begins and how he begins on the page makes comments about how he relates to these aspects. As he moves to the right he moves towards the future ... work to be done, expectations, aspirations ... Movement upwards symbolises gravitation towards the spiritual and intellectual spheres; movement down is a dive into the material, sub-human, subconscious spheres (one cannot help diverting here for long enough to point out that the word *dive* is used by Americans to represent just such a subterranean place!).

Thus the manuscript becomes a symbol of the writer's attitude to the past, present and future, to himself and others, to the spiritual, social, material, confused or clear, hostile or friendly, banal or sensible world in which he lives. And the moving pen of the writer becomes the symbol of his journey through the world, through life itself, as well as a symbol of his fitting the parts of his life (symbolised by the letters and words) around him. This may be done with ease and grace, or else the writer may display considerable resistance to this task – in which case his writing may show conflicting tendencies (as indeed most of us do).

Suffice it to say writing is not an aimless movement and even those who seek to disguise their motives give the game away by the very process of their concealment.

History

There is a marvellous account of the history of graphology in Renna Nezos' book *Graphology: The Interpretation of Handwriting* and those who are particularly interested can dive deeper there. Here is a potted version of what she and certain others have researched.

Since the word *graphology* comes from a Greek root (*graphe* = writing and *logos* = definition, in this context) it is fitting that Aristotle (*circa* 300 BC) was one of the first to make mention of disclosures gained through studying handwriting. The first graphology book (as far as we know) was published in Italy in 1622 but before the origins of graphology are attributed entirely to Europe it is as well to record that calligraphers must have been interested in its symbolism since they began to form shapes to interpret thoughts: Chinese brush painting is surely an early example of interest and respect in this sphere, as was the (much later) use of quills, which were deployed in the same way: to express essential artistry as well as meaning in writing. However, it is true to say that it is only since the scientific era that reason has dictated and delineated the theory of graphology as we now know it.

By 1830 there was a school of interpretation of writing in France, and by 1871 the intellectual Abbé Jean-Hippolyte Michon founded the Société Française de Graphologie. He was in many ways the father of Graphology (with a capital "G") since he devoted a lifetime to collecting thousands of handwriting samples and additionally wrote several books. The study continued to develop in France until the end of the nineteenth century, when Germany began to usurp the lead in this field. To this day the emphasis of interest lies on the European continent (particularly in France, Germany, Austria, the Netherlands and Switzerland). In England men of letters had upon occasion expressed their interest – including Shakespeare, Byron, Walter Scott and Browning – but it was not until well into the twentieth century that any real interest was taken other than in Europe (in whose universities there are several Chairs of Graphology – namely in France, Germany, Greece and Italy, where it is studied, as in Greece, in conjunction with a Law degree). At this time of writing (1989) graphology is still largely excluded from recognised schools of learning in English-speaking countries, although it is very quickly being put on the map due to the introduction of psychoanalytical knowledge to graphology which began in Zurich circa 1930 with Max Pulver's work and has been further researched and refined by Dr Paul Carton, René Le Senne and latterly by a pupil of Jung, Ania Teillard, who introduced depth psychology to graphoanalysis by applying Jung's four main functions of intuition, thinking, sensation and feeling, together with two attitudes, extrovert/introvert, and two tendencies: animus/anima and the persona (1980s).

Now that the extent and accuracy of graphological assessment is at last being recognised, headhunters and personnel departments are beginning to hire the services of graphologists – as are marriage bureaux – and it is becoming a very respectable profession indeed: so respectable that soon, no doubt, English-speaking universities will adopt it and claim they invented it.

How Graphology Works

All graphological analysis is based on the fact that there are about 250 signs or traits which have been detected in handwriting and it is the identification and compilation of these traits, as they are found in each individual's handwriting, which produces the analysis, usually in descriptive form.

Categorisation of the traits (according to Nezos each individual's handwriting contains about forty to sixty of these) is usually arranged under headings or categories which may include layout, dimension, pressure, form, speed, continuity, direction, and particular signs (Nezos). Other graphologists may sub-divide differently: Singer used sixteen headings including degree of connection (to what extent letters were joined together or not), regularity (whether the letter-size, slope and spacing are constant or not), and shading (whether the writing appeared to have been written by a brush or not), but they all amount to the same in the end.

Everything which is contained in writing is ultimately assessed and judged and once this evaluation stage is complete there remains the equally demanding task of compiling the evaluation into a coherent report. This is usually done under headings such as: personality, vocational skills, emotional indications, organisational ability, etc. From these examples of the categories which may constitute a graphological report it can be seen that there is no element of foretelling. However, if character is destiny, then graphological analysis could be thought to foretell the future in so far as it assesses potential. A child's school report could be thought to do the same.

For those who would like to know a few fundamental facts about how graphology works, handwriting is divided into zones and those zones relate to specific spheres of attention. The analogy of a tree is helpful in providing an understanding of the concept behind this zonal division of upper loops, middle letters and lower loops. The lower zone, corresponding to the roots or lower loops, is where we see the earthy traits such as interest in money, sex, sport, etc, the earthy materiality of life. The middle zone corresponds to the trunk of the tree or middle letters, and represents the to-ing and fro-ing of the day-to-day functions, the practical reality of life. The upper zone represents the ideals and aspirations, the spirituality of life. Obviously exaggerations in one sphere or another indicate a preponderance of interest in that sphere, or an aspect of it.

Slope of handwriting is another fundamental issue to be judged and again the analogy of the tree is helpful. If a tree has grown upright it has been unaffected by pressures from the environment: if its trunk slopes in one direction or another it indicates that an influence has been brought to bear on its growth, such as a prevailing wind or rocky, uneven ground. Upright (vertical) handwriting represents objectivity, impartiality, an ability to see both sides of an issue: it can also indicate detachment or even coldness. Handwriting which slopes to the right shows someone who wants to get out and meet the world half-way – an extrovert. Leftward-sloping writing shows withdrawal and the opposite trait – introversion. Both are adjustments to environmental pressure. Handwriting analysis becomes very logical when broken down in this way but it is probably appropriate, here as anywhere, to emphasise one basic immutable rule: NO ONE SIGN IS SIGNIFICANT OF A TRAIT. Each part must be judged in relation to the whole.

Signatures

People are fascinated by signatures and it is probably appropriate to say a little about them, but first to draw attention in respect to them of what has just been said: that they are just ONE SIGN.

The signature represents the "I" of the writer and as such it is notably revealing, especially when judged in relation to the rest of the writing. Any departure from the usual style which is seen in the signature (whether larger or smaller, more or less legible, or emphasised by underlining or embellishment) indicates that the writer has set himself apart in some way – he has *signified* himself for special attention. But what is his purpose – disguise, flamboyance, ambition, ease of execution? Nothing is simply judged in graphology.

Uses and Abuses of Graphology; The Ethics Involved

What would you get out of a graphological reading? Everything you need to know about yourself or another person. However, if your desire is to learn about another person, you may have to convince the graphologist that you have a right to such knowledge. Usually they will oblige if they feel reassured that you are not going to use the information to harm the other person. There is a very strict code of ethics in respect to graphological analysis.

Here is an example of how this code of ethics may work. A wealthy young woman who was severely handicapped attracted the attention of a young man who seemed utterly charming and who asked her to marry him so that he could look after her. She wrote to me (she had been a client of mine for some years) asking me to look at his handwriting because she did not know very much about him and he was pressuring her to marry him. Because of the important issues involved and our long professional association I had no compunction in agreeing to analyse his handwriting for her and I told her (with considerable regret) that in my professional opinion he was dishonest and, worse, a confidence trickster. Sadly she sent him on his way (he had been very good company) and I agonised over what I had done – until a few weeks later when one of the leading banks contacted her to see if she knew his where-abouts. She told the bank's investigator of my analysis and the detective then told her that the young man was wanted in several countries for misuse of credit cards.

This example is typical of the line most graphologists would take in respect to a person who is genuinely wanting to know more about an object of their affection. Which leads us to one of graphology's greatest uses . . .

Compatibility

Because the technique of graphology has so much to offer in respect to character analysis, it is the ideal tool to use for assessment when you are planning to spend a lot of time with another person, for one reason or another. Whether work or play, love or a professional liaison, an analysis of both your handwritings will indicate areas of agreement, disagreement and, more important, how you can resolve those differences. Looked at from this positive viewpoint (and not from the viewpoint of what is wrong with the other person) it is an invaluable tool for relating.

Modern Applications of Graphology

Just as one of the key applications of astrological principles to twentieth-century life has been its association with psychology, equally is this link benefiting graphology. Renna Nezos, who traces the association of the most important psychological systems with graphology in her above-mentioned book, says "you cannot become a graphologist until you know psychology. How else can you under-stand what you're seeing?" However, as Nezos points out, it is one thing for graphologists to understand what they are seeing, and another to label it, and this, she says, should never be done. The graphologist's job is to describe traits, not to suggest what the traits mean.

Nevertheless the graphological/psychological connection is one which is increasingly likely to involve students of graphology, and

Mrs Nezos, who founded the London Academy of Graphology in 1986, envisages corresponding complexity in the graphological courses available (her own is scheduled to develop from the three-year course to a four-year one), because of the widely-expanding scope of graphological work in the community. A further area of study will be forensic work (for example, where fraud is involved) because Nezos finds that the current standards of such work in respect to judging handwriting are often inadequate. What seems to be happening today is that graphologists are being asked to judge (describe) matters of increasing importance in terms of responsibility to the community, and in starting the Academy Mrs Nezos has recognised the need to improve standards of instruction, as no doubt will other graphological teaching bodies.

Choosing a Consultant

Addresses are given in Part 3 which will put you in touch with Graphological Societies in your area, who will have a list of members who are qualified to give analyses. Most members have particular interests such as vocational guidance, personnel selection, or personal work. Some like working with children, and such work can provide wonderful insights and guidance concerning the young, both from the educational point of view and from the problem (emotional/psychological, such as difficulty in relating, etc) point of view.

It is wise when ordering an analysis to tell the graphologist where you want the main weight of attention directed: it is no good being told about your career potential if all you want to know is why you do not seem to be able to find a partner! (Be prepared for some home truths.)

Most graphologists will wish to be paid in advance, that is, upon the ordering of the report. Again it is preferable to establish a rapport with any consultant you wish to use, so a telephone call may be more advisable than contacting by post. Although there is no logical reason why you should like your graphologist, it will help you to trust what they say.

Perhaps it is important to mention here that there are graphologists who work on a psychic vibration, in that the information they receive comes, at least in part, from the emanations given off by the handwriting and from their impressions as they study it. This is not, strictly speaking, true graphology (any more than cheiromancy is true palmistry) and if you find a consultant who is prepared to tell you what the writer was wearing or where they were sitting when they wrote the handwriting sample – or any other anecdotal material obviously derived from second sight and not from analytical deduction – then you have not got a scientific graphologist; you have got a psychic who is using the handwriting as a focus through which to funnel psychic ability. This may be very impressive, but it is important when you are choosing a consultant to understand what you are getting. If a person has a diploma, you can feel confident that even if the faculty of intuition is used, the theory of graphology has been grasped.

When to Use a Graphologist

It would be easier to suggest when not to use a graphologist! I analyse the handwriting of everyone with whom I come into contact, including bank managers, cleaners, even ships that pass in the night! It helps me to understand them, to avoid treading on their toes. I certainly would use it if I had an important relationship to assess, business or personal. And I would use it if I was experiencing difficulties with someone.

If I ran a business, large or small, I would *never* hire anybody without having the handwriting analysed first. Not only would it help me to weed out the applicants, but also it would be important from the point of view of understanding staff who are already employed or who might become employed in the future. Graphology can show as yet untapped potential.

However, there is a caveat to be mentioned in this respect. I for one do not believe that employers have the right to know about their employees' private lives and I restrict information to aspects of their handwriting which pertain to their professional life. For example, this could mean that I may comment about honesty, but it would not mean that I would comment about homosexuality –

unless, perhaps, I thought that it was going to directly affect his professional behaviour.

Personnel and Personal Selection: Graphology versus Other Methods

How well does graphology facilitate the tasks of selection and discrimination upon which it is increasingly being asked to report? Whilst it would be fair to qualify the following anecdote from Mrs Nezos with the observation that it depends on the graphologist, it none the less speaks for itself. The example she cites is an extreme one of a pattern which nevertheless repeats itself regularly.

"Let's say a company advertises for a position or a post and they get twenty-five or thirty candidates, which they filter first through either psychological tests or interviews and then send me a bunch of those short-listed. (Please note I don't advise them who to take on or not, I just describe the personality to their questions.) And again and again it happens that the first bunch they send me are found to be no good, so they send me another bunch, and so on. In this particular instance they had twenty-five applicants for a job and they kept sending them through to me until finally they were forced to send two they had completely rejected. In one of those two was their best applicant, a really brilliant young man. They hired him four years ago and I've been following it up because I'm always wanting to learn what happens in case I'm wrong. And he's doing brilliantly. Yet I discovered he was the first they rejected. He was introverted, a very discreet introverted person. He had a slight limp, perhaps it was that. I never meet the applicants so I'm only speculating but although this is an extreme case, the pattern repeats itself all the time: the successful candidate comes from the ones they had as a reserve."

Graphology and Health: Graphotherapy

Some graphologists believe that they can assess health in the handwriting, and I am inclined to agree with them, since any disease will show up as disharmony in the handwriting. Psychological disturbance is certainly likely to show up, as is stress, depression, fatigue, etc. However, some graphologists go so far as to say they can detect, for example, brain tumours and stomach ulcers and other physical conditions. Whilst I accept that there is a likelihood of this being the case in the future, I believe that more work must be done before the exact location of physical diseases can be pinpointed. Areas of malfunction can usually be seen (such as injuries to the spine affecting the legs appearing in handwriting's lower zone) but to be more specific requires the examination of many thousands of samples.

Graphotherapy is really a subject on its own. The contention is that to correct a negative trait in the handwriting will bring about a corresponding improvement in that area of the person under therapy. This may have validity as part of a therapeutic practice incorporating other techniques. My only observation is that when we as beginners start to learn graphology we all try to change the negative traits we have witnessed in our own handwriting, but after a while we give up and revert to our old ways! However what is set in motion is a long-term desire to improve ourselves brought about by the realisation that we have such-and-such a negative trait in ourselves and we really must do something about it!

Overview

Graphology is probably the most consistent and most acceptable source of information about people and the way they tick. It requires very little effort to obtain a piece of handwriting while it requires a great deal of effort to cast a natal chart or have a print of your hand analysed. As such it is a simple, quick and expedient source of personal information. It can answer a spot question taking one minute or provide deep psychological insight in a report which may have required hours of intense study. It can be used to amuse in parties but should never be used to abuse privacy. So the graphologist in these circumstances would have to be chosen with great care. (Graphology is not a parlour game, but since people cannot be stopped from using it in this way, they might as well try to use it honourably!)

Its use in the upbringing of children is probably on a par with astrology, whose use in this field is also invaluable. But while astrology may not appeal to some parents, they may be prepared to have their children's handwriting analysed.

More than any other of the social sciences, graphology is rapidly gaining acceptance as the valuable psychological tool that it is, both for self-knowledge and knowledge of others. I would recommend that everyone tries to get a smattering of graphological knowledge because it will help them in their everyday life more than they can imagine. That said, there are teach-yourself books suggested at the end of this chapter. Courses are also available through some, if not all, of the Graphological Societies listed in Part 3. Some of these will lead to diploma status.

All graphologists have to start somewhere, and for those who wish to test their interest and comprehension without committing themselves to buying a book which may not suit them, I cannot recommend more highly the articles on the subject by Peter Marshall which appear every month in the specialist British magazine *Prediction*.

The following are recommended reading but it should be realised that many of the finest graphological works have not been written in (or translated into) English. However it is the intention of the London Academy of Graphology to translate and arrange the publishing of many of the classics, so referral to them – address in Part 3 – may yield information and in time results.

Booklist

Beauchataud, G. *Apprenez la Graphologie.* J. Oliven, Paris 1959.
Nezos, R. *Graphology: The Interpretation of Handwriting.* Rider, London 1986.

Pulver, M. *Le Symbolisme de l'Ecriture.* Stock, 1953.

Roman, K. *Handwriting – a Key to Personality.* Routledge & Kegan Paul, London 1949.

Saudek, R. *Experiments with Handwriting* and *The Psychology of Handwriting.* Books for Professionals 1978.

Singer, E. *Graphology for Everyman* and *Personality in Handwriting.* Gerald Duckworth, London 1954.

Teillard, A. *L'Ame et l'Ecriture.* Villain et Belhomme, Paris 1966.

12
THE TAROT
Life's Picture-Book of Wisdom

A prisoner devoid of books, has he a Tarot of which he knows how to make use, might in a few years possess a universal science, and discourse on all possible subjects with an unequalled doctrine and inexhaustible eloquence. Eliphas Levi

In this scientific age in which we live, numinous and highly evocative picture-symbols such as those which appear on the Tarot-cards promote, more often than not, hysterical reaction. People simply "fear the Tarot" – they know not why – in much the same way that people fear "evil", or things that go bump in the night.

This popular fear – or call it a popular misconception – has very interesting and comprehensible origins, which I would like to explore later in the chapter once a little bit more about the Tarot is known. (What the Tarot is NOT will thus become all the clearer for being set against what it IS).

Background

As usual with all these ancient systems of divination, the origins of the Tarot are obscure, but some of the earliest surviving examples of the cards themselves are said to appear in museums in Venice and Paris, Italy and France having a very long history of special attachment to the Tarot, dating back, or so it is thought, to around the fourteenth century. Certainly the appearance of the cards even to this day looks mediaeval, but there are also other strange affinities – to Middle Eastern, Mithraic and even pagan Bronze-Age symbolism and to Semitism. This very diversity suggests that the Tarot has passed through many ancient cultures, or if we delve even more deeply, we could even suggest that the images of the Tarot precede the ancient cultures in that they are possibly mythological or even archetypal in nature.

It is well to steer one of the well-trodden middle courses, however, and start with the popular legend that they were said to have been invented for the amusement of Charles VI, King of France (1368–1422). (It certainly looks as if many of the early examples of Tarot packs were commissioned by royalty and aristocracy for use in gaming as well as for divining.) This legend may have sprung up because the Tarot we now have, said to be of Jewish origin, cannot be clearly traced further back than the reign of Charles VI, but it is possible that it is by no means the whole story, or even the begining of it, because the source of the Tarot has also been traced back to the Book of Thoth and that would bring us back in history to Ancient Egypt and to the time when Egypt was in danger of being conquered. The priests at that time were said to have decided to preserve all the remarkable occult wisdom known to that culture in a series of symbolic designs, and if this is so then the Book of Thoth, as the original source of the Tarot (Thoth was the Egyptian name for Mercury, god of communication) renders to the Tarot credence for being far more than just a collection of bizarre designs created for the amusement of the French aristocracy.

Indeed the science of hieroglyphics itself is thought by some experts to have been handed down to us in the Tarot, but in a modified and radically changed form. Hieroglyphics were based upon an alphabet in which the gods of the day (archetypal figures?) were represented in letters. Each letter had an individual idea attributed to it, and behind each idea was a number – the numbers were said to be in perfect harmony with the ideas. (We find similar echoes of numerical origins in astrology and the I Ching.)

Derivatives of the hieroglyphic alphabet, such as were carried forward in the Book of Thoth, were said to have been taken by Moses to his people. Moses was a scholar and well versed in the lore of the Egyptians, and he is said to have realised the importance of the information and guarded it jealously. Here we have another link which in turn leads us to the Kabbalah. But before examining this part of the labyrinth, another source leads us even further back into antiquity, to ancient China, where chronicler J. F. Vaillant claims that the Chinese have a series of drawings which "closely resembles the Tarot".* According to the Chinese (records Vaillant), this pictorial and symbolic way of depicting ideas originating from man's most fundamental experiences of life belongs to the first ages of their empire and as such predates any other record such as that of Moses carrying the information out of Egypt – and possibly belongs to the same epoch as that in which an understanding of the Zodiac began. One estimate ventured is 6,000 years ago!

Considering this complexity, no doubt those who write (of the origins of the Tarot) that they are lost in antiquity, are wise. However, to return to the trail of the hieroglyphic alphabet (the Book of Thoth) which Moses is said to have taken from the Egyptians – this, according to Eliphas Levi, another great exponent of the Tarot, "formed the great secret of his Cabbala ... for according to Sepher Yetzirah, it came from Abraham ... this alphabet we say is the famous Book of Thoth ... preserved to the present time under the form of that peculiar pack of cards ... called the Tarot".† It is certain that the twenty-two cards of the Tarot's Major Arcana (which comprises the essential Tarot) correspond to the number of letters in the Hebrew alphabet *and* to the number of paths in the Kabbalistic Tree of Life. (Again, we have echoes back to numerology and the special significance accorded to the number 22). Eliphas Levi goes on to say that he believes that "the Alphabet [Book of Thoth] is the original of our Tarot, only in an altered form. However the Tarot which we use now is of Jewish origin, and the types of the figures cannot be traced further [back] than the reign of Charles VI."

Back to Charles VI! And as such it becomes clearer why certain experts who have looked into the history of the Tarot refuse to recognise roots further back than where the trail actually ends.

Cherry Gilchrist, who has written a very good account of the Tarot in her book *Divination* (Dryad Press 1987), follows this view and puts forth a theory of her own which none the less links the

* Vaillant. *Les Romes, histoire vraie des vraies Bohemiens*, 1857.
† *History of Magic*, Paris 1860 and Rider, London 1957.

Tarot closely to the timeless language of mythology, as well as to religious symbolism and to folk music.

With all these links to ancient and respected cultures, it becomes curiouser and curiouser why the Tarot should evoke such horror from certain quarters of the Establishment. However, an examination of its imagery and the power of such imagery affords the glimmerings of understanding. Cherry Gilchrist explores this theme in her aforementioned book:

What is the Tarot? In modern Western society it has a colourful reputation – mysterious, dangerous, powerful, magical. It is associated in the popular imagination with psychic trances, with fortune-telling gypsies and pagan practices. Superstition has gathered around it and those who have dealings with the Tarot have been credited with undue influence over their fellow human beings. Much of this is myth, upheld by those who have probably never even held a Tarot pack and looked through the cards it contains.

The Tarot seems to sound deep echoes in the minds of men – unconscious echoes as if it is touching a nerve buried deep in a past racial memory. Jung has written that there is a group human consciousness in which are stored memories of all that has gone before in humankind – memories which may be buried, for all we know, in the nine-tenths of our brain which we do not consciously use. They may be the stuff of which our stranger dreams are made, the dreams where creatures and symbols emerge which are not now part of our daily lives. Kings and queens can play their part in that pageant of the night, as can dragons, snakes, strange prehistoric birds and many other potent images, all with the same timeless quality. Anyone who has woken from such a dream shaking with a nameless fear may begin to understand just why the Tarot images appear to have such power over us – they are "shorting across" the familiar parts of our memory to that which is buried deep in the racial memory: they are speaking to us in the pictorial language of symbols which predates the spoken word.

There may be another reason why the Tarot arouses such enmity in certain sections of the Establishment which is not quite so pretty. Since the rise of the patriarchal society and the age of rationalism, the irrational (often associated with the feminine – note the give-away term *feminine* intuition) has aroused repressive behaviour in those who are no doubt finding it hardest to suppress the feminine (intuitive, indulgent, feeling) sides of their own natures. Legendary characters like the domineering Mr Barrett of *The Barretts of Wimpole Street* (outwardly suppressing his daughter but inwardly suppressing what she stood for) illustrate this perfectly, as does Somerset Maugham's powerful character in *Rain*, the Rev. Stanley Davidson, who had such a Promethean struggle with his sex-drive (and eventually succumbed to it). This is the underlying principle which may in extreme cases occasion the desire to whack the Tarot down.

(Interestingly, there is a revival of such fanaticism right now from a minority of extremists in the Establishment sector and occult groups are being attacked as they were in the Middle Ages. I believe the revival of such attitudes may be to do with the realisation of just how much the public interest has grown in matters occult, an interest which is now refusing to be suppressed and so its suppressors are striving all the harder.)

Structure of the Tarot

Nowadays the Tarot consists of seventy-eight cards – twenty-two comprising the Major Arcana and fifty-six comprising the Minor Arcana – the latter most closely resembling the playing cards in use today with their four suits of clubs, hearts, spades and diamonds. In the Tarot these suits are called by a variety of names, the most common of which are Wands, Cups, Swords and Pentacles – relating in the same order as those mentioned above. There is only one difference and that is that there are five court cards in each Tarot suit and only four in our popular playing cards.

The Major Arcana are said to relate to the forces pushing and pulling us in our lives – those which may be construed as Fate or Destiny – the things we have to pit out wits and will against. The Minor Arcana are said to relate to the issues and events which arise as a result of the forces (inner or outer) impelling us, the things which literally put us at "sixes and sevens" – and which ironically are often represented by just those cards!

It is agreed by most experts that the original Tarot consisted solely of the twenty-two cards of the Major Arcana, and these are the cards which are structured to represent the journey of life, the Pilgrim's Progress. This early Tarot was the one linked historically with the Hebrew alphabet.

From roots such as this it is clear that the Tarot was never meant to be a disseminated collection of cards but a true book of life, even if in this instance its chapters have been separated into cards so that their true purpose could be better disguised.

Origins of the Name

As with all the lore surrounding this remarkable collection of cards, the origin of the name Tarot is also open to alternative speculation. On some of the earlier cards (and on some packs today) the back of them was covered by a series of crossed lines, a design called *Tarotee*. When Roman numerals were later introduced above these symbols, the game played with these cards was known as *Tarocchi* (in Italy today you may still buy Tarocchi cards from the newsagent in order to indulge in the gambling game still played with them).

However, Tarot authority Etteilla has a different idea. He says the name Tarot is derived from the Egyptian words *tar*, a path, and *ro*, or *ros*, meaning royal, which when combined means *royal path of life*.

J. F. Vaillant, writing in the same work as previously quoted, thinks the name comes from the great divinity *Astaroth, As-taroth*, and links this divinity with the Indo-Tartar *Tan-tara*, the Tarot, the Zodiac.

Yet another authority, Count de Gebelin, an eighteenth-century occult writer, said he believed the book derived its title from *taru*, an Egyptian word which means "to require an answer".

Take your pick! The origins of occult knowledge are never easy to uncover: possibly all the streams of thought about the origins of the Tarot's name had a common source.

How the Tarot Works

To suggest how the Tarot works is a bit like breaking down the structure of the solar system – we can only suggest some of the ways in which it might work.

The Tarot is read by a process whereby the cards are shuffled (usually by the querent) and then cut or selected (usually by the querent) and then those selected are dealt (usually by the interpreter) in a certain pattern or order. Sometimes the querent is asked to select the cards, but more often than not once they are cut they are in the hands of the reader or interpreter, who disposes of them as he/she sees fit. Some Tarot-readers read from the entire pack, but most work with remarkably few of the seventy-eight cards. Some (a few) do not even ask the querent to touch the cards at all, and it is a well-known fact that some Tarot-readers will undertake to do a reading in the complete absence of the querent!

This gives rise to all sorts of loudly-voiced misgivings on the part of the public, and it may be as well to try and find answers for these misgivings, even if they can only be hypothetical.

One of the biggest criticisms about this method of foretelling goes something like this: how can a pack of cards, randomly shuffled and barely (if at all) handled by the querent, possibly tell the questioner anything of relevance about their life?

Such critics tend unfavourably to compare the Tarot with other foretelling techniques, arguing that the principles behind astrology, for example, can be better accepted, in that an astrological chart *is* linked to the querent: it is a map of the heavens corrected to the time and location of their birth and as such may have some kind of synchronistic link with them. Palmistry is even more acceptable because it is based on a map of the living hand, and graphology is still more acceptable because the brain is guiding the hand which is using the pen. It is the Tarot which sticks in their gullets!

Of all the theories which attempt to get behind the Tarot's processes, the newest concerns one of the five senses, that of touch. In America it has been shown that the healing touch (sometimes called the therapeutic touch) does involve the actual transfer of energy from the one touching to the one touched. Furthermore, it has been observed that the recipient's brain-wave patterns actually change during the process of energy exchange (and for some time after) to synchronise with the brain-wave patterns of the one giving the therapeutic touch. This then is a powerful effect, and the fact that the healer is usually in some altered state of consciousness during the transfer of the healing energy may indicate a heightened awareness being present in the one and being transferred to the other.

Some psychics believe that all genuine forms of divination are in fact another manifestation of the healing process.* A querent comes with a problem and the consultant tries to help, to heal that situation and the person in it. This is not so far-fetched when we consider how popular psychology has become and how many people consider that going into analysis or going for counselling is a form of healing. We are getting closer and closer to the realisation that what heals the mind, heals the body.

Thus touch, and the transfer of energy in a mutual situation of heightened awareness, may be involved in some way with the process of a Tarot reading, where not only the consultant but the querent is in a highly-tuned state; the one because a psychic talent is being called upon, the other because a problem (usually emotional) is uppermost in their minds. Under these circumstances matters could be influenced which would not normally be influenced, and the transfer could be effected either through the physical process of touching the cards or through the psychological psychic process of the heightened awareness state of healing.

However, this line of theorising does not explain how the touch of either the querent or the consultant (or their joint awareness) can influence the selection of the cards. Nor does it explain how stunning results are got from the Tarot even when the querent is not present (however, the phenomenon of absent healing does come to mind).

Delving even deeper into the realms of possibilities, we cannot avoid the consideration that a sixth sense is very definitely operating, and that the reader is tuning in to the subject and the subject's

* See Chapter 7.

current situation, just as a healer tunes in to the condition of the patient requiring healing. If this is done, then would it not be comparatively easy to extract from the cards laid, themselves rich in the diversity of their symbolism, what seems to be of relevance to the querent? In other words the cards may be used as a mine of information, and that which is selected to be mined is the psychically-directed choice of the interpreter. This may be one of the reasons why it has been noted that for a good result from the Tarot reading there has to be a sympathetic bond between the card-reader and the querent. Surely another way of putting that would be to suggest that they are on the same wave-length? Which brings us back to the synchronising of the brain-wave patterns (as witnessed in healing and also in altered states of consciousness among groups).

Beginners and the Tarot

Whilst the previous descriptions of Tarot techniques and their undeniable effectiveness in gaining insights about one's life-situations do imply skill on the part of the interpreter, there is none the less overwhelming evidence to support the Tarot's efficacy for those who have gone out, bought a pack of cards, taken them home, read the brief instruction book included with most packs, and set about laying the cards, for whatever particular dilemma in life inspired their purchase. Remarkable insights are often gained.

But then another phenomenon may be occurring which is equally in danger of giving the Tarot a bad name. Whilst the first few readings by the beginner may seem remarkably relevant, subsequent readings often prove disappointing, and readings attempted by the beginner for family and friends can be disappointing too (or clearly the result of prior knowledge or vested interest).

This phenomenon, apart from being beginner's luck, is, I think, inspired by the initial impact of the cards. At first the information they give is so overpoweringly rich and yet so fundamental to the problem in hand, giving clues to the causes and effects of such problems, that the beginner's vested interest is overwhelmed by the concentration required to interpret the cards. However once this honeymoon is over, subjectivity begins to creep in, because new readers have not the training, not the body of knowledge, or the experience with the process of interpretation, to enable them to keep themselves out of it. It is difficult enough for practised readers to read for themselves – one so wants the outcome to be as desired – but nigh impossible for the new reader. Thus I would suggest that however effective the first few tries with the Tarot seem to be, a professional interpreter should be selected for problems of a major nature.

Choosing Your Tarot Consultant

It must by now have become obvious that the choice of Tarot consultant is of paramount importance. The reading is to be conducted with a highly evocative and symbolic medium (in fact one Tarot expert, John Christopher Travers, likens the Tarot to a venerable old man – who should be treated with respect) and the process is one in which all the power of the collective unconscious as well as your own personal unconscious is about to be stirred. It is extremely advisable not to plan to do very much before or after a Tarot reading (apart from taking notes) because you will be in a heightened state of awareness and should use the time to reflect upon your problem.

Making the Appointment

Unlike astrology and to a lesser extent palmistry, and certainly unlike graphology, Tarot readings do not require lengthy preparation or deliberation on the part of the interpreter, so they can be had on a more immediate basis.

This exactly suits the medium of the Tarot, which is at its best when used for matters arising. Suddenly you are offered a job, or suddenly you feel a proposal (or a proposition – much more likely these days!) in the air and you want to know the undercurrents, the forces at work below the surface.

The Tarot excels in such areas. John Christopher Travers, who writes for top U.K. occult magazine *Prediction* on the Tarot, says:

"The Tarot is a very strong aid to divination. It is also an aid to clairvoyance. It can reveal influences and circumstances, ways out of situations, and it can give advice. It is best used to answer questions, to answer things that are really worrying in life."

The Tarot, then, is the perfect medium for the chatter of life, the fine detail of life, detail which the astrology chart would rarely afford, nor the hand have the palmar surface to record. The Tarot deals with images which often link to actual people – kings and queens usually are the "kings and queens" in your life; knights are news-bringers and saviours of situations, just as they were of old when they rode through the forests rescuing people; pages are troublesome, amusing, lovable Puck-like creatures (often young people you know) who represent minor spanners in the works or harmless bits of fun or gossip. The Tarot is all so very logical when it is presented in this way.

In the hands of a good and wise Tarot-reader, a Tarot reading can tell you all that you need to know about a situation which has cropped up at that particular time in your life – but it will only tell you as much as you are ready to know, or as much as your Tarot-reader knows.

And this brings us to two other important issues: at what level should the Tarot be read, and at what level is the Tarot-reader capable of reading it?

There is no doubt that Tarot-readers work on vastly different levels. There are those with a genuine psychic gift who know little or nothing about the mythology behind the cards but will give you a very good reading about who and what is coming into your life and what sort of impact they are likely to have. They will probably even venture a description of those playing their part from looking at the cards selected ... and they could well be right at least in major instances.

Tarot-readers who are possessors of occult knowledge and who have probably studied psychology and alchemy and who are interested in the meaning and symbolism behind the cards, will not tend to read on the who's-coming-into-my-life level, but rather on the why-they're-coming-into-my-life level.

The guide in Part 3 of this book is to groups who will put you in touch with Tarot-readers in their group. But you should be aware that most Tarot-readers do not belong to groups: being highly individualistic people and often loners, they are not usually disposed to belong to groups. One of the better ways to seek out a good interpreter is to find out who writes on the subject (although this is not always a guarantee of expertise in reading – although a good writer always has a referral system). A better way possibly is to buy one of the specialist magazines in your area and use your own intuition to guide your choice.

John Christopher Travers believes that a good Tarot interpreter will be able to interpret at all levels but will tailor the reading to the needs of the client.

It's quite clear that if a teenage girl comes in having love problems, she's not going to be interested in the deeper values, the spiritual matters. She wants a superficial reading, and so you skate over the deeper imponderable meanings of the cards because of the kind of attention she has at that particular moment. She may be a very intelligent girl but she is having a certain kind of problem at that time and you have to relate to that problem.

Then somebody else may come in and you immediately behold that there is a wonderfully-developed personality. They are not interested in superficiality, this has got to be a deep reading, and the depth and profoundness that comes out makes you wonder at the incredibility and to feel quite shattered and drained afterwards. So there are so many different levels and nobody is the same coming for a reading. There's a totally different approach and needs to be, even if the same cards come down for each person.

Time and the Tarot

One of the most vexed questions of all in the realm of foretelling is: how good is this system with telling me WHEN an event predicted will actually take place? What is the accuracy?

Sometimes the Tarot can be amazingly accurate: certain cards in the pack are known to be linked to certain time-intervals ...

but, as always, results are variable. It really depends on how inevitable a predicted situation may be. If you are heavily committed to a certain path of action, such as being deeply in love (and that love is reciprocated) the Tarot will usually tell you pretty clearly when the matter is likely to develop one stage further! (Or if there's likely to be a delay.) If you have broken the law and robbed a bank, the Tarot will be sure to tell you when conviction is imminent! But on matters which involve others' actions, or matters not ready to be judged (even if they seem just as inevitable) the Tarot can be quite definite as to the nature of the outcome, but incredibly vague as to when the outcome might occur.

I remember going to consult a Tarot-reader when a question of choice arose in my life, a choice which I felt to be unavoidable (in other words no choice!). The cards laid indicated that I did have a choice and that if I made the choice I was considering, I would have to pay the price: they even told me what the price would be. I went ahead and nothing happened for several years, until remorselessly, one by one, the predictions came to pass over a four-year period. When I returned to the Tarot-reader at the end of that period to tell her of her uncanny accuracy in construing the cards, which had just come true to the last card laid – and could I please have another reading – she looked at me and said: "No wonder I've given up the Tarot. Four years is too long to wait for the next fee!"

She had used a method whereby the enquirer selected the cards and she (the reader) put them in order – which bears thinking about.

On the question of time, if it is of the utmost importance, it is always advisable to seek information from more than one source – and then marry the accumulated evidence together.

A Question of Attitude

When going for a Tarot reading, it is important to keep an open mind. The first time the Tarot is laid for each individual is not necessarily the best . . . a rapport has to develop between the reader and the querent and it is a rapport which may take time to ripen.

The Tarot is alone in this, since with other techniques the first time can often be the best.

Many people ask Tarot-readers what the cards mean and how they arrived at the things they say. This is the equivalent of asking your watch repairer to tell you in detail how he repaired your watch and what were his reasons for taking the steps he took in order to do so. There is nothing more infuriating to a Tarot-reader than to be asked to explain the logic of something she has probably not logic-ed out at all. Sasha Fenton puts it very well in *The Fortune-Teller's Workbook* when she asks this question of her readers: "Can you understand the amount of responsibility that a professional needs to have and the split-second decisions that he needs to make with every reading he does?"

So please do not take your reader apart to see how she ticks!

Learning the Tarot

Learning the Tarot is like learning a new language, exciting at first, but very tedious and painstaking. Madeline Montalban, whose articles on the Tarot became an ongoing classic in *Prediction* over a twenty-year period, used to say that learning the Tarot was a feat of memory which would seldom be equalled. Each of the seventy-eight cards has several meanings (or ways of being interpreted) and when these have been learned the job is only half-done, because meanings of reversed (upside-down) cards must then be learned. (Some Tarot-readers do not bother with this: others insist upon it.)

Then the cards must be learned in conjunction with other cards, so the permutations are possibly endless.

However, this should not deter the enthusiastic amateur who can always keep her work-book near her when she does a reading (I always do). A good way to start is to read several authorities (the booklist at the end of the chapter is designed for this purpose) and from them to compile your own work-book of meanings. This is one of the best ways to learn – because you are forced to condense and hence deduce what the experts are trying to say. The other way is to practise – on yourself and on your long-suffering family and friends. If you are a good story-teller, that also helps – not because you are literally "telling stories" but because a narrative gift is all-important for interpretation.

Lately, many adult education centres have begun to teach all sorts of subjects relating to the occult, and if enough people request such courses, the more likely they are to oblige. Finally, there is always the directory of relevant societies in Part 3 of this book, although it must be said that it will prove very much more difficult to find instruction for the Tarot than it will to find instruction for the more standardised techniques – which is why some suggestions have been made here.

The Outcome

What does the average person stand to get out of a Tarot reading? Are the results as reliable as with astrology, palmistry or graphology?

The answer has to be no. A Tarot reading can be anything from sublime to ridiculous: how and when it will work and when not is beyond explanation, just as its symbols are often beyond words. One thing to remember is that the Tarot never lies: yet why, if it never lies, does it sometimes refuse to tell the truth? One can only put forth theories, and one of the theories which is worth considering is the attitude of the querent – yourself. It is just possible that querents get the reading they deserve. This is not to imply moral judgment but rather an absence of commitment.

Of course this sort of comment, which attributes part blame to the querent when things go wrong, drives the Tarot's critics to distraction. That is like blaming the observer in the science laboratory when the chemical reaction does not take place. But the concepts of quantum physics are beginning to shake even those bastions of belief: for it has been shown that the observer *does* influence the result of the experiment. So if the observer wants a certain result (or does not want it – however subconsciously), that is if he has not got a genuinely open mind, it is just possible he may get the result he has influenced. Even this concept is not so far-fetched if you think about people with green fingers (therapeutic touch with plants?) or mechanics who seem to have a way with engines.

So I leave you with this thought: we might be more powerful than we think – which means we might even choose our Tarot-cards by just thinking about our problem!

Booklist

Butler, B. *The Definitive Tarot*. Rider, London 1975.

Gray, E. *The Complete Guide to the Tarot*. Studio Vista, London 1970.

Huson, P. *The Devil's Picture Book*. Abacus, London 1972.

Logan, J. (and Montalban, M.). *The Prediction Book of the Tarot*. Blandford Press, London 1983. (Jo Logan has done a very good job of condensing Madeline Montalban's 20-plus years of writing about the Tarot in *Prediction* but nothing can equal Montalban's original articles and for those with access to back issues of *Prediction* I would highly recommend that they are read in this way as well.)

Sharman-Burke, Juliet & Greene, Liz. *The Mythic Tarot*. Rider, London 1986.

Waite, A. E. *The Pictorial Key to the Tarot*. Rider, London 1974, 1986.

Woudhuysen, J. *Tarotmania*. Sphere, London 1981.

13
PHRENOLOGY
Study of the Mind

*Our normal waking consciousness . . . is but one type of consciousness,
whilst all around it, parted from it by the flimsiest of screens, there lie
potential forms of consciousness entirely different.* William James

Phrenology, the delineation of character and potential by an analysis
of the shape and proportions of the head, was very popular in
the last century and in the beginning of this one, after which it
unaccountably lost popularity.

However, it is due for a well-deserved revival, probably under
the aegis of modern medicine, owing to the development of new
scientific techniques which are enabling the head to be scanned in
respect of the mental activities associated with particular areas.

This sort of research has not hitherto been possible because of
the thickness of the skull – electroencephalograms of the brain
have merely indicated brainwave activity, but the more subtle
electrical energies associated with various types of thinking and
spheres of mental activity could never be mapped in relation to
their exact location in the head because the currents so detected
would only be picked up wherever the skull was thinnest, or where
there was the least line of resistance to the tiny currents reaching
the surface of the skull – such as where two bones of the skull
joined (there are no less than twenty-nine bones in the skull).

All this may seem to have little to do with "having your bumps
read", but in fact this is exactly the territory that is starting to be
mapped scientifically, and the areas which have already been
mapped are co-inciding with traditional phrenology's perception of
them. What seems amazing is how the founders of phrenology
knew which areas of the brain represented which faculties when it
has taken all the skills of modern technology to confirm and
rediscover these principles.

The Principles

Phrenologists contend that each "bump" or part of the head is related to a particular kind of mental activity (such as calculating ability or combativeness), so if one part of the head happens to be large or well-developed in proportion to other areas, then that faculty will be one used a lot by the person under study. For example – and this is a descriptive phrase of which most people will have heard – someone with a "bump of location" usually has a highly developed faculty of finding their way around.

There are two main principles on which the science of phrenology rests, that of the localisation of mental function and of the belief that size is a measure of power, other things being equal. It is those principles and how they came to be discovered that is the subject matter of this chapter: that and the interesting nature of the research which is beginning to establish just how vital a part the mind plays in our organisation of the dimensions of time open to us; present, past and future. As scientists are just beginning to realise: the brain is merely an instrument of the mind. But first the history.

History

Phrenology began in the West in 1758 with the birth of an Austrian boy, Franz Gall, later known as Francis Gall. Franz Gall was a budding anatomist (later to become a doctor) who started to take wax impressions of his friends' heads while still a schoolboy. One of his companions was very good at finding birds' nests and this stimulated Franz's sense of wonder. Later he was to compare the bumps on his friend's head with bumps on the heads of fellow medical students who were also good at finding their way around. (He found each bump was over the left eye and called it the bump of locality.)

He isolated twenty-six more bumps, each one associated with a particular faculty of mind, by which time he had an enormous collection of three hundred human and animal skull casts.

In 1823 he visited England and brought with him his vast collection of heads cast in wax, as well as portraits of outstanding people, all of whom, according to Gall, owed their success to a particular bump on the head. He lectured to packed, excited audiences of the medical and social élite.

Suddenly phrenology became fashionable, and his students as well as himself became very well-known. One of them, George Combe, published a book in 1828 called *The Constitution of Man*. It sold 17,000 copies in a year, whereas Darwin's *Origin of the Species* took 15 years to do the same. Gall himself had also written a book which was to become *the* classic phrenology text book and was much-read by the medical profession: *The Anatomy and Physiology of the Nervous System in General and the Brain in Particular*.

Famous personages who had their bumps read included George Eliot, Balzac, Karl Marx and Baudelaire, and in America President van Buren submitted to the phrenologist's gaze. (He was pronounced to have large faculties of self-esteem, benevolence and approbation.)

What was happening in Victorian England and to a lesser extent elsewhere was really a revival of Greek thought. The Greeks believed there were four basic personality types: sanguine, phlegmatic, choleric and melancholic; dispositions arising from excesses of either blood, phlegm, or black or yellow bile in the body fluids. The phrenologists' beliefs were not dissimilar. They classified people into three main temperaments: vital (sanguine, well-padded); motor (tough-minded, muscular) and nerval (volatile thinking) types. They too linked these conditions with excesses or deficits in certain body fluids amongst other indications.

By the mid-1850s, largely due to the influence of one or two key antagonists (Lord Macaulay was one of them), phrenology began to fall into disrepute and by the end of the nineteenth century it was discredited intellectually but nevertheless still enormously popular, possibly corresponding to the popularity of astrology today.

Nevertheless there was still sufficient interest to see the inauguration of the British Phrenological Society in 1943 and one of its most illustrious members, the aptly-named Miss Frances Hedderly, carried the torch (and wrote an excellent book called *Phrenology, a Study of the Mind*) until the Society's liquidation in 1967, when their valuable collection of books was divided between the University of Cambridge and University College, London.

What remains of the practice of phrenology now continues in the East, where it began, but the tide is turning as once more medical scientists interest themselves in mapping the mental functions.

Phrenology: Science of the Mind

From its history it can be seen that phrenology is far from being on the fringe of fortune-telling – in fact it is a study which has always been based on measurement and observation, and as such it can rightly be called a science. The word phrenology itself comes from the Greek *phren*, meaning "mind" and *logos*, "science" – put together "the science of the mind".

However this should in no way detract from its inclusion in this book, because what is likely to happen is that more and more of these so-called fortune-telling arts, as they come under improved and more open-minded techniques of scientific scrutiny, will be included in a whole body of study relating to the psychology and personality of man. And they will be just as acceptable and important as other branches of science are today.

Many years ago the popular poet of his time, Alexander Pope wrote: "The proper study of mankind is man." Science has been so busy looking at man's technological achievements throughout the nineteenth and twentieth centuries that it has almost forgotten to look at man. But the revival of interest in psychology during this century and the corresponding advance in the understanding of the power of the mind to influence events has made men of letters realise that instead of looking outwards they should be looking inwards.

Thus, I predict, very soon you will once more be able to go and have your bumps read in order to discover what your mental capacities are and what your weak and strong points may be, in order that you can cultivate those faculties which will help you along the particular road you wish to travel in life. Character is destiny – or a large part of it.

It may be difficult to believe that anything can be done to alter the pattern as delineated on the head, but in fact, just as the lines on the hand can and do change when there has been a corresponding change in attitude within the person, so, we are assured by phrenological researcher Johann Spurzheim, do the bumps on the head. Spurzheim mentions two cases: the first is that of an English client of his, who, in order to test this hypothesis, periodically had casts of his head made and then directed his close attention to some new mental pursuit for five years. On comparing casts over several five-year periods, the first and last casts were found to differ so greatly that it was difficult to believe that they had been made from the same head.

This concept of changing something as apparently unchangeable as the skull shape does not seem too far-fetched when the anatomy of the skull is understood. Its 29 bones allow for plenty of readjustment along their junctions. It is the brain which determines the shape of the skull and not the reverse.

In the unborn child the brain is formed long before the skull is formed, and during youth and early adulthood the skull readily accommodates itself to the developing mental organs within. In spite of its apparent hardness, bone is living matter, and when the brain develops in a particular area, because mental activity corresponding to that part is being exercised, then the bone thins underneath that area, and new bony matter is formed on the outside.

Phrenology teaches that known differences of character correspond to certain variations in the size, shape and condition of the skull. For example, men who have become famous thinkers and philosophers usually have proportionally large heads with high, broad foreheads. Men with little or no reasoning power have small, flat heads with slanting foreheads. Picture in your mind the drawings and photographs you may have seen of prehistoric man such as neanderthal man, whose thinking faculties had not yet developed, and you will have a clear picture of what is meant.

Phrenologists believe that it is not only the bumps on the head that are significant, but the size, width and shape of the head. To ascertain the head's dimensions for the purpose of analysis they take no less than 13 measurements after which they compare these with a table of average measurements in order to determine where the differences lie.

The forty-two separate brain centres which the phrenologists have identified are then reviewed and classified according to the subcategories of the three temperament types and the seven major function-groups or regions of the brain.

Frances Hedderly, whom I once had the privilege to interview when she was well into her seventies, said that after taking the necessary measurements and notes (which will include colour of the eyes, colour and consistency of the hair and shape of the nose) she would often put her notes away for days until suddenly she was aware of how to interpret them. "Did this imply an intuitive faculty?" I asked at the time.

Miss Hedderly's answer could well have applied to any kind of analysis done by means of one of the physiological patterns discussed here: "First you must study your subject and build a foundation of knowledge. Then, and only then, can you allow your powers of intuition to help you interpret your observations."

A phrenological analysis is a complex compilation of such observations, exclusive to each individual. Nevertheless there are some general traits and indications, and here are some of the pointers to them which she gave me:

● Executive energy is shown if the head is long from the ear forward (because the centres which signify good executive powers such as reason, observation and capacity to acquire knowledge are all found in the front of the head).

● A large jaw denotes strength of character and body. (Those with double chins have a more easy-going, vital temperament.)

● A large nose is fortunate, because it corresponds with the capacity to endure both physical and mental hardships.

● Rounded or high foreheads indicate good reasoning and intuitive powers.

Miss Hedderly pointed out that traits that have something in common are usually grouped together, so that the 42 separate areas of the brain can be subgrouped into 7 zones or regions such as the Moral and Ethical Region, the Self Perfecting Centre, and so on.

One very graphic way for a beginner to study the variations in head protuberances or bumps would be to study the more obvious differences between various peoples of the world and what they mean. For example, the average Caucasian head is high, with a relatively bulging forehead and moderately developed back-head compared with other peoples, such as the African Negro. This indicates that we have evolved in a thinking, reasoning and techno-logical society where such traits are of benefit. Those of us who are very religious or moral or who have spiritual leanings have large top-heads as well, and it is fascinating to note that again this falls in line with esoteric teaching, that the crown chakra (an energy zone situated on the top of the head through which energy ex-changes occur) is said to be our contact with the spiritual realm.

The African Negro, whose heads are more elongated from front to back and whose back-heads are usually very well developed has on the other hand developed in a society where instincts are of paramount importance in the role of survival and those, according to phrenologists, are located at the back of the head. It is interesting to see that this predominance is changing where and as the Negro adopts the lifestyles and values of Caucasian society life. As the phrenologists say, the exercise of any talent leaves its mark on the skull.

Modern Science and Phrenology

During the past few decades the brain has been subjected to a tremendous amount of scientific observation, as awareness slowly grew that brain wave patterns were associated with varying states of mind. One of the pioneers in mapping these fields was scientist and mystic, Dr Maxwell Cade,* who together with Geoffrey Blun-dell built an advanced form of encephalogram known as the Mind Mirror. With this Maxwell was able to observe four different kinds of brainwaves: Betawaves, normally in the range of 14–26 cycles per second which is the waking rhythm of the brain: Alpha, between 8 and 13 cycles per second, signifying relaxed awareness; Theta,

* Cade, C. Maxwell & Coxhead, Nona. *The Awakened Mind*. Wildwood House, London 1979.

between 4 and 7 cycles per second, and associated with drowsiness, but also with access to unconscious material; and Delta, between ½ and 4 cycles per second, and primarily associated with deep sleep.

This exciting work has thrown light on the whole concept of altered states of consciousness such as are thought to be displayed by mediums, clairvoyants and healers in the healing process and, on a mass scale, in native festivals such as those featuring ecstatic dances or walking over glowing coals, all of which presupposes a state of mind which transcends bodily perceptions such as pain and fatigue.

Dr Cade worked with holy men of the East who had in some cases spent their lives training their minds through meditative and other techniques and found that the most disciplined of these could control their brainwaves completely, and also synchronise the left and right hemispheres of the brain. The left side of the brain is known to be the site of logical and sequential thought, categorising and speech, whilst the right side of the brain, sometimes known as the dark side of the brain, concerns itself with the detection of colour, shape, design, music and abstract concepts associated with the creative urge.

With such differences in function between the left and right hemispheres of the brain, it is rare to find an individual whose brainwave patterns show synchronicity between left and right. It requires a measure of mental control and wholeness of mind which is not normally associated with man.

Other scientists have carried on the work of Maxwell Cade and, with the aid of even more sophisticated devices such as the magnetoencephalogram (MEG) which measures not just brainwaves but the more delicate and sensitive magnetic fields produced by the brain's activity, researchers are beginning to have a clearer understanding of the links between higher mental processes (for example: the forty-two spheres of consciousness as described by phrenologists) and underlying brain activity (as indicated by brainwaves). Throughout history it has been intuited that the mind, although it cannot be perceived and is an intangible concept, nonetheless exists and furthermore governs the brain. But in the age of realism men began to doubt the predominance of the mind and to believe that the brain, the only tangible factor in mentality, was the origin of the mind. Now the work of Wilder Penfield and others has resulted in there being a return to traditional thought on the matter: the brain is seen as the hardware, to use computer terminology, and the mind as the software. Thus the brain is the physical instrument through which the mind acts.

Of course this concept gives rise to the question: if the mind exists without the brain and without any tangible evidence of its existence, then is it perhaps immortal? Does it persist after death? And what relation might it have to the ancient concept of the soul?

All these questions are as yet unanswerable in their entirety, however we can at least approach the edges of the darkness which surrounds such issues and throw light on what *is* known. For example, this concept, the theory that something *might* exist which survives death is examined in the next chapter of this book which is devoted to the research of yet another medical scientist and psychiatrist, Dr Raymond Moody, who has written the popular books *Life After Life* and *Reflections on Life After Life.* (Researched from his case histories and documented observations of those who have been, because of illness or accident, to the gates of death and back.)

Meanwhile, the case for phrenology strengthens: the more we can know about the workings of the mind and the brain, the more we can know about altered (some would say heightened) states of consciousness which have always been associated with clairvoyance, healing, mediumship, telepathy and prophecy.

Booklist

Combe, George. *The Constitution of Man.* 1828.

Gall, Francis. *The Anatomy and Physiology of the Nervous System in General and the Brain in Particular.*

Hedderly, Frances. *Phrenology: Study of the Mind.* L. N. Fowler, London 1970.

14
AROUND THE ULTIMATE CORNER
Evidence to Remove Fear

How do we know that the living are not dead and the dead living?
Euripides

One of the major reasons why people fear predictive work is because
they fear being told something dire. To many, the ultimate "dire"
prediction would of course be death, or serious illness with its
threat of fatality. I have discovered that people stay away from
foretellers in their droves because of this unspoken dread, and it is
because of this discovery that I have decided to write a chapter
about death, a chapter which I hope will plant at least a seed of
reassurance in some hearts.

Death has been the subject of some very intensive research
in recent decades, largely through the medium of near-death
experiences (NDEs) which are becoming increasingly prevalent
due to ever-improving medical ability to resuscitate those on the
brink of death.

As a result a considerable body of empirical research has been
gathered not by psychics and mediums, who have been observing
the death phenomenon for years and have always had their own
views about it, but by highly qualified doctors and scientists working
sometimes in resuscitation wards and sometimes within psychiatry
(the latter for the purpose of rehabilitating attempted suicide cases).
Some of the researchers have worked with desperately ill children
who have been near death. Whilst the researchers agree that their
findings would never satisfy science because they can never be
replicated (for obvious reasons!) they say that the vast numbers of
cases they now have on record, plus the similarity of their experiences, can no longer be discounted as a body of evidence. That,
and the fact that it has been estimated by Gallup that such experi-

ences have been shared by 35 per cent of all Americans who have had a close brush with death (some 8 million people – and the figures are much the same for the U.K.) mean we are talking about an experience that has been shared by a considerable number of people. Why then have we heard so little about it?

One of the best-known researchers in this field is an American, Dr Raymond Moody, who wrote a best-seller about his research called *Life After Life* (currently printed in thirty-four languages).

Dr Moody is a psychiatrist with a doctorate in philosophy. He is also Professor of Psychology at West Georgia College. So he could hardly be referred to as fey. Dr Moody became interested in NDEs while he was still a student, when one of his professors told him about a local psychiatrist who had had an amazing near-death experience. Moody went to a lecture on the subject by this man and was so impressed with his sincerity that he started collecting cases of his own, which was quite easy as he was in medical school. By the time he graduated he had material on eight such experiences and what struck him was the consistency of them: namely that everyone who had had a NDE returned transformed, and without any fear of death.

They all described similar experiences during their NDE: of being out of their body, often of looking down on their body while it was being resuscitated; of moving through a tunnel into a place of light and beauty, and of being met either by relatives who had died or by a being of light.

They also described going through a life review in which everything they had said, thought or done in their lives flashed before their eyes; of a sensation of being outside time, so that a moment seemed eternal; and lastly of being told (or in some cases deciding) they had to come back and being very reluctant to do so. Each person described the tremendous feelings of love that were around them, and they brought those feelings back with them and subsequently led lives which were in many ways enriched by what they had seen.

One of the researchers, a Dr Bruce Greyson, who works as an emergency psychiatrist at the University of Connecticut, deals with suicides on a daily basis and he has collected over 1,000 NDEs from them. Suicides are notable for trying again and again but Greyson finds that those who have NDEs as described above hardly ever try to commit suicide again, because they realise that life has a purpose and that they are here to fulfil that purpose, whereas those who do not have NDEs frequently try again.

Another colleague, Dr Melvin Morse, a paediatrician at the University of Washington School of Medicine, has for years investigated children who have had NDEs. Children have less cultural conditioning than adults, yet they describe exactly the same experiences . . . being out of their bodies, going through a tunnel, being met by the being of light (which they often call God) and of the feeling of love and happiness. Dr Morse has recorded his findings in three articles published in the *American Journal of Diseases of Children* (hardly the psychic press). Moody, who has also interviewed child NDEs, says that one interesting aspect of their experiences is that they frequently describe themselves as adults during the time that they are out of their bodies. Moody suggests that this could indicate that the "spirit itself is an ageless entity that finds itself housed in an ever-changing body".

Here is an excerpt of one child's NDE as published in *The Light Beyond*, a sequel to *Life After Life* (see booklist):

This happened when I was eleven. I got a new bike for my birthday. The day after my birthday I was riding my bike and I didn't see a car coming and it hit me.

I don't remember getting hit but suddenly I was looking down at myself. I saw my body under the bike and my leg was broken and bleeding. I remember looking and seeing my eyes closed. I was above.

I was floating about five feet above my body and there were people all around. A man in the crowd tried to help me. An ambulance came. I wondered why the people were worried because I was fine. I watched them put my body in the ambulance and I was trying to tell them it was fine but none of them could hear me. I could tell what they were saying. "Help him," someone was saying. "I think he's dead but let's go to work," said someone else.

The ambulance drove off and I tried to follow it. I was above the ambulance following it. I thought I was dead. I looked around and then I was in a tunnel with a bright light at the end. The tunnel seemed to go up and up. I came out on the other side of the tunnel.

There were a lot of people in the light but I didn't know any of them. I told them about the accident and they said I had to go back. They said it wasn't my time to die yet so I had to go back to my father and mother and sister.

I was in the light for a long time. It seemed like a long time. I felt everyone loved me there. Everyone was happy . . . I didn't want to go back. I almost forgot about my body.

When I was going up in the tunnel two people were helping me . . . They told me I had to go back. I ended up back in hospital where two doctors were working on me . . . I saw my body on this table and it looked blue . . . One doctor put paddles on my chest and my body bounced up.

When I woke up I told the doctor I saw him put the paddles on my chest. I tried to tell my mother too but no one wanted to hear it. I told my teacher in class one day and she told you [Moody].

Moody believes one of the main reasons why so little is said by people who have NDEs is because of anticipated ridicule. But anyone reading statements like this would find it very hard to dismiss them as fantasy.

Nevertheless critics say NDEs are either caused by the drugs given sick patients or they are the brain's way of compensating for the fact that the person is near death, or even that they are a form of mental illness. Moody systematically examines and dismisses these and several other criticisms and anyone interested in the detail of this can read it in *The Light Beyond*. Moody has always said that it was never his intention to support any belief one way or the other, merely to present the anecdotal evidence as he recorded it. Since candour has a way of making its presence felt and there is any amount of it in the NDEs reported, only the most cynical would suggest that several highly qualified doctors in key medical and teaching posts throughout America would conspire to trick the world.

Where does this leave us? In his book Moody comes to several conclusions: that death is not the end, that life does go on in another dimension (some NDEs actually describe the feeling of being in a dimension outside time and space) and that our fears of death are groundless if the experiences of NDEs are anything to go by.

Psychics of course have been saying this for years. Owen Potts, who has sat with two people who died, says you can actually see the moment when the aura moves away: "I call it aura, life force . . . as soon as that moves away you can have out-of-body experiences but you're still linked. But of course at death it moves away never to return. The body is left like an empty shell."

David Bingham says much the same: "The body is like an empty container." David Young describes the dying process as the aura geting weaker and weaker. "When you know a person's ready to pass into the spirit world you can see it actually fading . . . as soon as they leave their body it's gone."

Sometimes even non-psychics report a whoosh and something shimmering leaving the body as death occurs. Moody says nurses sitting with the dying frequently report such happenings and a very down-to-earth friend of mine reported a similar experience when sitting with her dying father. "I looked away for a moment and in that moment he died. As I looked back towards him I saw a shimmering silvery shape forming about his body and suddenly it whooshed up and out through the ceiling."

Moody's NDE cases sometimes report trying to stop resuscitators from working on them (they also report, word for word conversations held in resuscitation rooms, sometimes to the extreme embarrassment of participants). One woman overheard a conversation which took place in the hospital lobby while she was being resuscitated in another room. She saw her brother-in-law being approached by a business associate who asked him what he was doing in the hospital. "Well I was going out of town on a business trip," said the brother-in-law, "but it looks like June is going to kick the bucket so I'd better stay around and be a pallbearer."

A few days later when he came to visit her (reports Moody) she told him, "Next time I die you go off on your business trip." (June reported to Moody that he turned so pale she thought he was about to have an NDE.) These experiences are peppered throughout Moody's books, including other material of a more serious nature in which NDEs report that they know that they are all interconnected. One woman put it this way: "I had a total, complete, clear knowledge of everything that had ever happened in my life . . . not only my deeds but every single thought AND its ramifications on everyone else. I realised I affected everyone and everyone affected me . . . we were all connected."

NDEs come back valuing two things above all else – love and knowledge, because they say they know that they are the only two things we can take with us.

Owen Potts believes that those who die young just have a small task to complete in the life they are leading. He cites cot deaths as an example of this. He believes that every affliction, every misfortune has a reason. David Bingham says that although he is sometimes shown a potential accident or illness in a person's life which could be fatal, he knows he would never be shown one which fell into the "tight options" (that is, inevitable) category. Potts has this to say on predicting death: "I can honestly say I've never been given an exact date of death but I've had people come to me who have had their death predicted and I'm pretty sure the person they saw didn't get it either, in fact they were giving false information and also ensuring their own power over the client. I don't think it's anybody's place to play God, ever."

With that we return full-circle to my own experience which started all this research and has ended with such a reassurance about that ultimate change in life. I am also equally convinced that although there are good and bad in the prediction world as there are in any profession, the only time we are told something negative is when we can do something about it. And even the ultimate "bad" prediction – death – looks increasingly as if it may be good news in disguise. However, Moody noted that NDEs never tried to hasten their own death, quite the reverse; they realised their lives had a definite span and a definite purpose.

One of the greatest philosophers and psychologists of our time,

Jung, had a near-death experience after a heart attack. Later he described it in this way:

> What happens after death is so unspeakably glorious that our imaginations and our feelings do not suffice to form even an approximate conception of it.
>
> Sooner or later, the dead all become what we also are. But in this reality, we know little or nothing about that mode of being. And what shall we still know of this earth after death? The dissolution of our timebound form in eternity brings no loss of meaning. Rather, does the little finger know itself a member of the hand.

Of course all this implies a belief in reincarnation – how else would apparently negative lives have any meaning? But that is not the subject of this book.

Booklist

Anything by Edgar Cayce on the subject of reincarnation.

Cerminara. G. *Many Mansions*. Spearman, London 1967.

Coxhead, N. *The Relevance of Bliss*. Wildwood House, London 1985.

Cranston, S. L. and Head, J. (eds). *Reincarnation in World Thought*. Julian Press, Crown Publishers Inc., New York 1986.

Grey, M. *Return from Death*. Wildwood House, London 1985.

Greyson, B. and Flynn, C. P. (eds). *The Near-Death Experience*. Charles C. Thomas, Springfield 1984.

Jung, C. G. *Modern Man in Search of a Soul*. Routledge & Kegan Paul, London 1961.

Moody, R. *Life After Life* and *Reflections on Life After Life*. Bantam, U.S.A. 1984. *The Light Beyond*. Macmillan, London 1988.

Ring, K. *Heading Towards Omega*. William Morrow, New York 1984.

Stern, J. *The Search for the Girl with the Blue Eyes*. Doubleday, N.Y.

15
HELPING YOURSELF TO YOUR FUTURE
Self-Help Techniques

The media put our work into the corner with party games. Harry
Gullefer, Hon. Sec., Society for the Study of Physiological Patterns

Successfully helping yourself to your future is likely to depend on
two key factors: your own preparedness to learn how to incorporate
a foretelling facility in your life, and the preparedness of those who
are able to provide the facility. As of now the standards of the latter
vary too greatly to be called anything like a profession: rather do
they consist of a loose agglomeration of those who are gifted
sprinkled with those who are unscrupulous. Until the facility for
foretelling is taken more seriously and incorporated into the structure of society and not left entirely on its fringe, this circumstance
will prevail and the quality of foretelling results will continue to
suffer as well as to depend on all too few gifted individuals.

One of the ways in which improvements can be brought about
is by public demand, both for more divination services and for
higher standards among them. Everyone's knowledge needs to be
improved.

The media could lead this movement if they so wished by setting
up investigatory and educational programmes and features instead
of perpetuating the same tired formulas which usually focus on the
more sensational aspects of foretelling. The media are also fond of
setting up dialogues with disbelievers in which foretellers are forced
to justify themselves in an extremely hostile environment. Yet how
can critics even begin to understand, let alone judge, the work of
foretellers unless they learn a little of how they go about their task?
In other fields, people have a smattering of knowledge: they know

about health because there are medical programmes on television; there are money programmes which inform about money. Yet that most compulsive area of interest, foretelling in its various aspects, is either neglected or treated in the same old sensational way as before, partly because the decisions of how to treat it are made by people who do not know the field. (It is amazing how many newspaper, radio and television executives believe themselves to be authorities in this field – or otherwise hold such strong views about it that they preclude unbiased presentation.)

Another way in which the public can help is by educating themselves, by learning a little bit about how foretelling works, by incorporating divination in the regular pattern of their lives, at least in some small way. And, if possible, by keeping records of how well a chosen method performs. Another phenomenon witnessed throughout this field is credulity, which is the other side of the incredulity coin, the persecution mania from which this whole area also suffers. Both are extremes and both are unbalanced.

People who have investigated those with special gifts which embrace foretelling, have come to the conclusion that such gifts are within us all to a greater or lesser degree. But they lie dormant. Paying attention to these stirrings of the sixth sense within us may contribute to raising the "water table" of human consciousness in this way. The rest of this chapter is devoted to suggesting some ways in which this might happen, ways which may help you to get in touch with the diviner within you – your own knowledge of the future, of how things are likely to be with you.

As I explained in the Foreword, this book is not designed to cover ground already covered by many other books, that is, to instruct and show how foretelling techniques work for DIY reasons: however, I am briefly outlining four methods which may introduce the field to those who would seek it out.

Dreams

Some societies, reputed to be atavistic or behind the times, revere their dreams and gather in groups to relate and re-enact them each day.* They believe that dreams give access to a world beyond the dimensions of the one in which we live. Certainly there is ample evidence that dreams can foretell the future, which suggests that in the world which dreams can enter time does not exist.

Dreams can also be used to gain insight into our deepest conflicts, conflicts which may be motivating us in directions not in our best interests. Both Freud and Jung studied the dreams of their clients intensively, the better to help and understand them.

To record dreams, one needs to have pen and paper at hand by the bed, and to religiously write them down before arising. But how does one get to grips with material which seems so wispy, so strange and so unintelligible?

One of the best ways of getting to the bottom of dreams is by taking each role in the dream and personalising it: making it speak, preferably to others in the dream. This not only applies to people who may have featured in a dream, but objects such as a snake, a club, a river – whatever material arose.†

To achieve this re-enactment it is definitely best to be alone. (I well remember when I started this technique I decided to act out a dream in which my mother had appeared. As I subsequently took her part and then mine and verbalised the subject of the dream, we ended up having a shouting match which could have been heard three blocks away!) So be alone.

Try to set up as many chairs as there are dream components. Keep one for the overviewer – the one you will drop into when you want to ask a leading question of a dream character or direct the action. Let the material extend itself but keep true to the dream and its theme. (Remember not to mix your voices and not to be tempted to stay in the same chair to reply to something which has

* The Senoi, who live in the central highlands of Malaysia, teach their children to respect and interpret their dreams and to re-enact or actualise them. The Senoi are remarkable in that there is no violent crime, armed conflict or mental illness within their boundaries. It is thought that the dream-work they practise produces a considerable degree of psychological integration. You can read more about this in Lyn Webster's book, listed below, and about the theory in Arnold Mindell's work.

† Fritz Perls wrote *Gestalt Therapy Verbatim* and the theory behind this process can be found in this excellent work.

been said – you will get your characters mixed up if you do.)

After a bit of practice you will be amazed what conflicts you have been burying, what corners of your life you have been avoiding, and what insights you get – providing you go with the flow and do not see yourself as being foolish.

This is a far better method of interpreting your dreams than buying a book of dream meanings and lumping yourself in with everybody else who has had a similar dream. Dream symbols do have generalised significance among humankind, but each dreamer uses them in such a highly individualistic way that a symbol can mean the opposite of the commonly accepted meaning.

Counsellors trained in psychology will always help you with your dreams if you really cannot get to grips with them yourself (some are mentioned in Part 3) and also there are some book titles suggested at the end of this chapter which go more deeply into dream theory than I have the space or the knowledge to mention here.

Even if you do not plan to work on your dreams immediately, do start recording them: it is a very well-known fact that people who trouble to record their dreams have more and more of them which they can remember. They are also more likely to have visionary dreams, dreams about their future which could help them to plan visionary projects.*

Dowsing or Divining

The concept of dowsing was introduced in Chapter 8, and although the best dowsers are much-sought-after professionals, it is their general belief that anyone can be taught to dowse. Anyone can make a pendulum, too, with which to dowse – a cotton reel

---

* There are many examples in history of inventors dreaming the solution to a problem of design, etc, which had been exercising their conscious mind. Perhaps the most famous is that of Kekulé, who dreamed how the benzene ring was formed; but there are many others such as Elias Howe, who dreamed the construction of the needle which enabled him to invent the sewing machine, and Niels Bohr, who dreamed the model of the atom, which led to the foundation of atomic physics.

suspended from a length of cotton has been used, as has a plumb-bob or a fisherman's sinker. Theoretically anything will do that weighs about two ounces and is symmetrical around its vertical axis. The ideal string length is about three inches.

The purpose of making a pendulum is to tap into that other part of your consciousness which "knows" in the sense that was explored in Chapter 8. However, this "sense" does not communicate in language – it lies beyond language – its facility lies in indicating whether an answer is in the positive or the negative. Thus careful questions have to be formulated which measure up to the simple requirement of getting a "yes" or a "no".

Dowsers use this skill all the time; it is the same whether they use a divining rod or a pendulum. (A divining rod indicates a positive when it bends or spins.)

Those who want to use a pendulum need to work out whether it indicates "yes" when it swings clockwise or the reverse. This is done by asking it a number of questions to which you know the answer. Many people find that "yes" is clockwise and "no" anticlockwise, but there is no fixed rule.

Like every skill, it is one which requires practice and some people seem to be better at it than others. Basically, you have to practise until the manual part of the skill becomes automatic. Dowsers will also tell you that the state of mind is all-important, too – it has to be a kind of relaxed focusing on what is being sought after – exactly the same kind of state in which Einstein solved his mathematical equations; the state which Dr Maxwell Cade has described as "diffused awareness".

Dowsing can afford you the answers to many questions, from ascertaining what may be good for you to eat and what not (try not to allow your likes and dislikes to intrude), to where to find a missing object (by dowsing over a map of the suspected area).

Those really interested may find that their local society, such as the British Society of Dowsers (address in Part 3) holds beginners' classes. They are well worth attending, because you will then be shown how endless are the practical applications of dowsing in daily life.

Distinguished dowser Tom Graves has written an excellent book on the subject (see end of chapter) which is as down-to-earth in its advice as the skill which he practises. This is a good beginner's source. Those who are interested in dowsing for health reasons may want to read other books as well which concentrate more on that aspect; the Radionics Association address is the one to write to for medical dowsing booklists and information.

The I Ching

The I Ching, or Chinese Book of Changes, is one of the classic foretelling oracles ideally suited for those who wish to divine for themselves. Oddly enough, Tom Graves suggests in *The Diviner's Handbook* that the I Ching, and even the Tarot, might be tools for tuning in to the dowsing instinct in all of us.

This is not so far-fetched when it is considered that the I Ching is based on a system of yang (active) and yin (passive). In fact in dowsing the opposite of the active response (yes) is more of a neutral (passive) than a "no", so the two are extraordinarily alike in principle. However, the I Ching, although structured on this binary principle (as are computers), has become more complex, as indeed are the more highly-evolved forms of dowsing. Yet they are still based on this opposite-pole principle.

To the ancient Chinese this system of two-ness held the secret which lay behind all change: that first there is one event or happening in life, then out of it a compensatory (other) thing eventuates. Like the seasons, yang and yin alternate, and in alternating over long periods of time they combine and recombine to make up the complex structure which we call our destiny. Soap operas are built on this principle, as they trace the destinies of their characters through generation upon generation of acting and reacting to each other.

The structure of the I Ching oracle is composed of sixty-four hexagrams or life-situations (giving a total of 4,096 answers or permutations) and these are said to cover the whole of life's possibilities. They are most often selected by throwing three coins six times to construct the hexagram pertinent to the enquirer's question. Once the hexagram has been constructed, the appropriate text can then be read which will give insight into the subject of the enquiry. One expert, Raymond van Over, described the I Ching as "a device whereby the enquiring mind of the questioner can find road signs that can lead him to his destined place in the world".

The I Ching is not easy to consult. Although one of the standard books which contain the Oracle (see end of chapter) will give you clear instructions about how to "throw" your hexagram and how to frame your questions (most important), the actual texts (readings) are both obscure and difficult to follow. Modern translations and interpretations are available, but to my mind they should only be read in conjunction with a standard work.

Readers may feel entitled to ask why I have suggested three DIY techniques all of which require tremendous effort on the part of the enquirer. This is because in making the effort you are less likely to influence (become subjective about) the interpretation. In choosing one system which works with visual images (dreaming) one which works with the intuition (dowsing) and one which works on a binary system (the I Ching) I am hoping that your answers will originate from that very part of the brain which psychics and gifted foretellers use, which is definitely not the logical, thinking, rational, overriding side – the side modern education conditions us to use.

The Runes

The Runes consist of 24 ancient Runic alphabet symbols, plus one blank, usually etched on stone or wood, which are thrown (or cast) and then interpreted. This ancient method of foretelling is said to have been devised by the Norse God, Odin, who hung himself upside down from the sacred tree Yggdrasil, where he stayed suspended for nine days, during which time he reached a stage of enlightenment. He then found the original runes among the roots of the tree.

Users of the Tarot will be familiar with Card No. 12, The Hanged Man, which depicts Odin, suspended upside-down under a tree, and the card itself is said to indicate self sacrifice. It is one of the cards of the Tarot very few people understand, fearing the hanged-man aspect of the image, but in fact the expression on the face of the god is very peaceful, even blissful, and the message is that the sacrifice is a voluntary one for the purpose of acquiring something of greater value, in this case "foresight" or the ability to divinate, an ability with which the god Odin is essentially associated.

The legend of Odin is in fact linked mythologically with the Roman god, Mercury (in Greek mythology, Hermes; in Egyptian parameters, Thoth), which brings the two techniques, Tarot and Runes, even closer together in their origins (although masters of each devotion might hotly dispute this!). Furthermore, both systems employ similar techniques - a number of symbolised life-options, in the case of the Tarot represented by cards, and in the case of the Runes represented by the twenty-five Runestones.

However, here is where the similarities end: for it is said that Runes, to be effective, should be hewn and marked by the user, who must either cut the necessary twenty-five pieces of wood from a tree (first asking the tree's permission), or fashion the symbols from soft stone, such as limestone or slate. (Pebbles can also be used). These are then marked with the relevant symbols and kept in a bag with a drawstring.

The simplest method of casting the Runes is for the enquirer to dip into the Rune bag and pick out whatever number of runes is needed for the particular spread chosen. Alternatively the Runes are laid out face downwards, swirled by the enquirer and then picked.

Layouts vary but one of the most popular is the clockface representing one month of each year. Some Rune readers use this twelve-stone spread to represent the twelve astrological houses, which is mixing their predictive metaphors a bit. However, when it is considered that what they are doing is using a form of concentration to reach that area of their brain/mind which is associated with intuition, an area that is definitely not associated with language (because that would immediately divert consciousness to the thinking function) it can be understood just what the strange Runic symbols are achieving. (The pictorial images of the

Tarot serve the same function, directing consciousness to the "dark side of the brain".)

Runes can be used either to secure a general reading or to ask a specific question. Like every other form of foretelling they are really best-used in the hands of an expert (known as a Rune-master), but it is definitely possible to use Runes personally, providing this is done in conjunction with a good interpretative written guide. Such a guide can be found in Derek and Julia Parker's book, *The Future Now* or in Sasha Fenton's book, *The Fortune-Teller's Workbook* (see booklist at the end of the chapter). In many ways the Runes comprise one of the best methods of self-divination since the Runic letters are so unfamiliar in form and therefore do not evoke any pre-conceived notions which may get in the way of genuinely intuited information.

There is only one caveat with consulting the Runes and that is "ask a silly question and you will get the answer you deserve". In this respect the Runes share with the Tarot the propensity to deal summarily with superficiality, i.e. to evoke the trickster side of the god. When this happens the answer so given can be very misleading indeed.

Why Not the Tarot for DIY?

Although the Tarot may be easier to use than the I Ching, I do not believe that it should be used as a self-divination technique – the pictures are too evocative: they have come to mean things to most of us which inspire preconceived ideas when we see them. I am not alone in my belief that the Tarot should not be used for self-divination; here are John Christopher Travers' views on the subject:

I do not like the idea of anybody sitting down and doing a Tarot spread for themselves, for the simple reason I think it's far too easy to misinterpret and misconstrue and particularly to think oh well, that means so and so, but I'm going to ignore that because I think it should be something else for me. And almost turning the meaning of the spread inside-out because it relates to what you want to know and not to what is actually there for you to know. Whereas if you were reading for somebody else you would be totally objective and wouldn't take into consideration whether it was what the person wanted to hear or not. You would simply deliver the goods.

Essentially, that belief expresses the whole direction and purpose of this book: it is an attempt to help people to find ways to discover their future which may not be foolproof, but are hopefully self-proof.

Booklist

Dreams

Bro, H. H. *Edgar Cayce on Dreams.* Paperback Library, N.Y. 1968.

Coxhead, D. and Heller, S. *Dreams: Visions of the Night.* London 1976.

Faraday, A. *The Dream Game.* Penguin, London 1976.

Jung, C. G. *Memories, Dreams and Reflections.* Collins and Routledge & Kegan Paul, London 1963 and *Synchronicity. A Causal Connecting Principle.* Routledge & Kegan Paul, London 1972 (this for more general applications) and similarly *Man and His Symbols.* Picador, London 1978.

Mindell, A. *Dreambody* and *Working With the Dreaming Body.* Routledge & Kegan Paul, London 1984, 1985.

Webster, L. *Dream-work.* Dryad Press, London 1976.

Divining/dowsing/radionics

Dowsing

Anything by Tom Graves but in particular *The Diviner's Handbook.* Aquarian Press, London 1986 and *Dowsing: Techniques and Applications.* Turnstone Books, London 1976.

Anything by T. C. Lethbridge (publisher Routledge & Kegan Paul).

Medical dowsing (radionics, radiesthesia)

Baerlein E. and Downer, L. *Healing with Radionics*. Thorsons, Wellingborough 1980.

Wethered, V. *An Introduction to Medical Radiesthesia and Radionics*. C. W. Daniel 1957.

I Ching

Blofeld, J. *The Book of Change.* N.Y. 1966

Hook, D. F. *I Ching and its Associations* and *The I Ching and You.* Routledge & Kegan Paul, London 1973.

Lui, D. *I. Ching Numerology.* Routledge & Kegan Paul, London.

Over, R. van. *I Ching* (Original text by Legge edited by van Over). New American Library, New York 1971.

Wilhelm, R. *Translation. I Ching.* Routledge & Kegan Paul, London 1951.

Runes

Fenton, Sasha. *The Fortune-Teller's Workbook.* Aquarian Press, London 1988.

Parker, Derek & Julia. *The Future Now.* Mitchell Beasley, London 1988.

PART THREE

DIRECTORY

In the following pages you will find a series of guides which will aid you in your search for the appropriate outlet to suit your plans, be that outlet a consultant for your first session, a school in which you can learn your desired subject, or other means by which you can garner information and understanding.

The Directory part of this guide is by no means comprehensive – it is extremely difficult to get information about arcane subjects such as these from external sources of enquiry, even if those enquiries have originated from a country as steeped in interest in matters esoteric and occult as Britain. Which is why, besides offering specific names and addresses to enable anyone to make a start, there are also guidelines offered as to how general lines of enquiry may be conducted. In many ways this book has been designed as a guide to the guides, and this chapter is no exception.

Sample Methods: A Safecracker's Guide to the Occult

As any good safecracker will tell you, if you can crack one safe you can probably crack others, so here are some formulas for extracting information (some of which have been recapitulated in summary form from Part I) in the event that you do not find what you are looking for in the Directory.

1. Buy a local or national magazine which specialises in subjects of this nature. Try to select the most up-market one you can find because it would appear that nearly everybody in this field is trying to move (and hence advertise) up-market. Perhaps sadly, they do not want to be associated with fairground fortune-telling any more.

You should find a wealth of advertisements for groups, societies, etc, in your field of interest and many of those groups, if applied to, will have names of experts in your area. (Obviously you will not write to an Astrological Association for the name of a psychic and vice versa . . . unless of course you're desperate . . . of which more later.)

2. If this avenue proves unyielding, try looking for advertisements in the personal column of a women's magazine. As above, the same rule will apply: the more up-market the magazine, the more established (and pricier) the expert. However, most reputable magazines do require some kind of reference from their advertisers, so you *may* be assured of some kind of quality: after that it is up to you to select from the wording of the advertisement the expert who may appeal to you. Basically, if you like the approach which a person has used to set up an advertisement, be it simple, humorous, or apt, etc, then its appeal should indicate that you are on the same wave-length. It is important to let intuition have free rein in this area as it may save you from working through all the options.

3. Write to the author of a book which you admire on your chosen subject and ask for referrals or advice.

4. Start asking people you know if they have heard of anyone. (Unless you know your source of information very well, it is advisable not to ask if they have consulted the person themselves: people are very funny about this most private aspect of their lives.) Personal recommendation is the best kind of referral you can get, provided you respect the person doing the recommending, but do question them as closely as you feel you can: your standards may be more exacting than theirs.

5. If these techniques and their resultant overtures fail to secure an appropriate expert in your chosen field, either you will have to change horses, or you will have to try abroad and get a postal or taped reading. (Which is not to be discounted: better to choose an A-grade expert and have a good postal reading than have your second choice with a less-desirable outcome.)

6. If, after making all the above efforts, you have not achieved anything like satisfaction, you will have to consider the remote possibility that either you are in the wrong place or it is the wrong time to be seeking such information. But before you reach that conclusion, you are advised to leave no stone unturned to get to

your share of the truth, and there are plenty of suggestions here to help you.

Directory

Always send a self-addressed envelope and stamps or international mail vouchers with any request for information – most of these organisations work on a shoe-string budget. You will note that there are many more astrology network addresses than for the other physiological patterns such as palmistry and graphology, or for the ESP techniques. This is because astrology has really caught on and has become enormously popular. This is partly due to exciting research backing up some tenets of astrology but not entirely. Graphology is also very scientific but outside Europe is nowhere near as popular.

If there is no address for your chosen outlet, it does not hurt to write to another address given here for that country or area and respectfully ask them for referrals. The occult field is very small and most experts know of each other.

Astrology (General) U.K.

ASTROLOGICAL ASSOCIATION. *Hon. Sec. Angela Cornish. P.O. Box 39 North P.D.O., Nottingham NG5 5PD.* The Astrological Association is a national association of astrologers, publishes a journal and a newsletter (the latter containing information about local and regional groups which may be a valuable source of information about consultants in your area). They also publish news of events, seminars and workshops and will furnish names and addresses of members.

ASTROLOGICAL LODGE OF LONDON. SAE to *BM Astrolodge London WC1N 3XX.* Founded by fathers of modern English astrology Alan Leo, historically the Lodge is the parent body of both the Faculty of Astrological Studies and the Astrological Association. Meetings are held every Monday at 6 Queen's Square, London WC1, and special seminars are mounted. Might be able to help with names of practising members in or near London.

BRITISH ASTROLOGICAL AND PSYCHIC SOCIETY. Details from *21*

Warnham Court Rd, Carshalton Beeches, Surrey SM5 3LY. BAPS will provide a list of consultants in all of the fields of expertise which they cover, not just astrology. (Although this largely consists of astrologers and psychics, there are certain other experts on their lists, including palmists, numerologists, and card readers. They also have a very talented sand reader.)

MAYO SCHOOL OF ASTROLOGY. Offers a list of their qualified consultants. (See address under next section.)

FACULTY OF ASTROLOGICAL STUDIES. Also offers a list of their qualified consultants. (See address under next section.)

Astrological Information/Education Groups

URANIA TRUST. The Trust is an important new centre for astrology in the U.K. and you can write to them for all queries of an astrological nature. They will furnish a list of U.K. schools and consultants and also available is an international astrological handbook (with directory). (SAE + large envelope for any queries to *396 Caledonian Rd, London N1 1DN.*) The Trust also has a library and runs research and other seminars.

ADVISORY PANEL FOR ASTROLOGICAL EDUCATION. SAE to *Sec., 21 Warnham Court Rd, Carshalton Beeches, Surrey SM5 3LY.* APAE is a co-ordinating group composed of two representatives from each of the main astrological organisations and schools in Britain. It also has some information about local education authorities' courses.

FACULTY OF ASTROLOGICAL STUDIES. SAE to *The Registrar, Rita Lambert, 29A Sussex Rd, Haywards Heath, Sussex RH16 4DZ.* Generally recognised as being the most outstanding teaching body of astrology anywhere in the world. It runs certificate, intermediate and advanced courses in astrology both by correspondence and through evening classes and seminars in London as well as introductory summer schools. Correspondence courses only, SAE to *BCM, Box 7470, London WC1 3XX.*

COMPANY OF ASTROLOGERS. SAE to *6 Queen Square, Bloomsbury, London WC1 3AR.* Runs a wide range of courses, classes, lectures and seminars and a summer school. It seeks to update astrological practice in line with modern trends, such as its increasing association with psychology.

Astrological Schools U.K.

ENGLISH HUBER SCHOOL OF ASTROLOGY (In association with API Switzerland; see under Europe). SAE to *P.O. Box 9, Totnes, Devon TQ9 5YN*. This is the English branch of Bruno and Louise Huber's influential organisation and emphasises the link between astrology and psychology. It runs good correspondence courses which focus on the counselling aspect of astrology.

CENTRE FOR PSYCHOLOGICAL ASTROLOGY (CPA). *P.O. Box 890, London NW3 2JZ.* the CPA is run by Liz Greene and Howard Sasportas and many other fine tutors. It concerns itself with the study of astrology in relation to Jungian depth psychology. Not for beginners!

MAYO SCHOOL OF ASTROLOGY. SAE to *Alvana Gardens, Tregavethan, Truro, Cornwall TR9 9EN.* Founded by author Jeff Mayo, the school offers correspondence courses at both certificate and diploma level and issues a list of their qualified consultants.

INSTITUTE FOR ASTROENERGETIC STUDIES (IAS). SAE to *Glenview House, IRL Portsalon, Co Donegal, Eire.* Offers a comprehensive computerised chart calculation service (very good for beginners) as well as a 5-year course for advanced students.

Specialist Astrology (U.K.)
Horary Astrology

Horary Astrology is enjoying a revival, and well it should, because it has very special abilities, such as the facility for judging the outcome of an event or meeting, or for finding missing objects or persons. It is discussed in more detail in Chapter 9, but for those who may have skipped across from Part 1, this little re-cap is to indicate how and when you should consult an horary astrologer. For those wishing to be put in touch with an horary astrologer or wanting to learn about this fascinating branch of astrological divination there are two schools in the U.K:

QUALIFYING HORARY DIPLOMA COURSE. (2-year diploma course). SAE to *Mongeham Lodge Cottage, Great Mongeham, Deal, Kent CH14 OHD.*
THE MEONEN SCHOOL (12-lesson course). Prospectus from *73b Dresden Rd, London N19 3BG.*

Astro*Carto*Graphy

Founder Jim Lewis has introduced this system to astrology whereby an individual's astrological data is co-ordinated with their location. Apparently some places are luckier for us than others and it is a good idea to know where in the world the lucky sites may be: if we cannot relocate there at least we will be happy holidaying there – or so the theory goes. Astro*Carto*Graphy also gives an insight into how living in a certain place might affect you. This is a fascination, especially for those who sense they could be luckier elsewhere. You need to know your exact time of birth to really avail yourself of Astro*Carto*Graphy. SAE to (U.S.A.) *P.O. Box 959 El Cerrito, CA. 94530.* SAE to (Australia) *Shop 22, 202 Pitt St, Sydney 2000* or *19 Kellet Grove, Kew 3101 Victoria* or *19 Thomas St, Croydon, S.A. 5008.*

Medical Astrology

For those interested in obtaining insights about health through astrology there is no referring association as such but there is a newsletter and applying to them with SAE may produce names of consultants. Write to *Medical Astrology Newsletter, 4 Balcastle Gardens, Kilsyth, Glasgow G65 9PE.*

Astrology

Europe

Belgium

FÉDÉRATION ASTROLOGIQUE BELGE/FABEF, *20 rue de Grand Cerf, B-1000 Bruxelles, Belgium.*

France

INSTITUT ASTROLOGIQUE DE FRANCE. *133 rue St Dominique 133 F-75007 Paris.*
BIBLIOTHEQUE ASTROLOGIQUE. *8 rue de la Providence, F-75013 Paris.*
INSTITUT ETUDES ASTROLOGIQUES. *29 rue de l'Héronnière, F-44000 Nantes.*
FÉDÉRATION FRANCOPHONE D'ASTROLOGIE. *134 avenue Jean Jaures, F-75019 Paris.*
ASTRO-PSYCHOLOGICAL PROBLEMS: The Schneider Gauquelin Research Journal. Not an organisation as such but a publication which may help if your interest lies in this aspect of astrology. Write to *B.P. 317, 75229 Paris, Cedex 05.*

Germany

ASTROLOGISCHE STUDIENGESELLSCHAFT. *24 Olendand, D-2000 Hamburg, Federal Republic of Germany.*
DAV (Deutscher Astrologen-Verband). *Merzhauser Strasse 145-B, 7800 Freiburg, Federal Republic of Germany.* This organisation maintains an information data bank and holds conferences.

Italy

LINGUAGGIO ASTRALE. As before, another publication which may help. SAE to *C.I.D.A., Via Panascall, 10138 Torino, Italy.*

Netherlands

ASTRO-KRING. SAE to *362 Leyweg, 2545 EE, the Hague, Netherlands.*
Astro-Kring is not an astrological association, it is a magazine and
newsletter (international exchange) and as such they may contain
advertisements or may service enquiries for locals wanting consultants. They also hold conferences.

AESCLEPIOS SCHOOL OF MEDICAL ASTROLOGY. They offer a four-
year course in medical astrology for Dutch speakers. Write to
*Vakschool voor Medische, Astrologie Asclepios, Singel 54, 1015 AB
Amsterdam, Netherlands.*

Scandinavia

The organisation Cosmos and the magazine *Alternative Key (Alterna-
tiv – Noglen)* is a treasure house of information about many esoteric
subjects. It is listed in the section to do with PSI contacts and ESP.

SAMMENSLUTNINGEN AF FAG-ASTROLOGER. (A leading institute of
astrology.) SAE *to Baldrianvej no 21, 2900 Hellerup, DK.*

KLASSISK & ESOTERISK ASTROLOGISK FORENING. SAE to *Mannavej
6, 2615 Brondby, DK.*

SCANDINAVIA/NORWAY ASTROLOGIST FORUM. This is a magazine
specialising in astrology which will have contacts at: *Box 7667
Skillebekk, N-0205, Oslo, Norway.*

Spain

REVISTA ASTROLOGICA: MERCURIO-3. A Spanish astrological publication, and also the centre for the Spanish Astrological Association.
SAE for help or subscription to *Apartado 92.001, 08080 Barcelona.*

Switzerland

ASTROLOGICAL PSYCHOLOGY INSTITUTE (API). Bruno and Louise
Huber's founding organisation for API. SAE to *Rutistrasse 4,
Postfach 614, CH-8134 ADLISWIL.*

INTEGRALES ASTROLOGISHES FORSCHUNGINSTITUT AG. *24 Chemin
des Dailettes, CH-1012 Lausanne.*

U.S.A.

NCGR (National Council for Geocosmic Research, Inc). *26W Susquehanna Ave, Baltimore, MD 21204-5278. U.S.A.* This organisation has 27 chapters around the U.S.A., 6 non-geographical special interest groups such as Helio, Financial/Mundane, and an active education programme with teaching and certification. They publish 12 member letters, 4 journals and one news magazine per year and would certainly have a network of astrologers from coast to coast. SAE to the above address.

AFAN (Association for Astrological Networking). *8306 Wiltshire Blvd #537, Beverly Hills CA. 90211.* This organisation holds conferences, works to improve astrology's legal status and public image.

ISAR (International Society for Astrological Research). This organisation maintains an information data bank, holds conferences, etc. *P.O. Box 38613, Los Angeles CA 90038-0613.*

ASTRO-CONSULTING SERVICES. Top consultant astrologers in the San Diego area have grouped to provide one-to-one consultations. They are affiliated to Astro Computing Services in that they can avail themselves of these varied calculation programmes, depending on your need. See address under Computerised Astrology section.

The superb astrologer, Ingrid Naiman, does a correspondence course in medical astrology. Write to her at *395 Alejandro Street, Santa Fe, New Mexico 87501, U.S.A.*

Canada

FCA (Fraternity for Canadian Astrologers). Publishes newsletter and holds conferences. Write to *The Membership Secretary, 13155 24th Ave., Surrey, B.C.V4A 2G2 Canada.*

Australia

FAA (Federation of Australian Astrologers). This is a national body setting guidelines for ethical practice, and researching into the different methods of astrology. They offer certificate and diploma examinations. With 500 members Australia-wide, they would have excellent referral potential. General enquiries to *National Secretary, P.O. Box 179 Coburg 3058, Victoria.* Alternative address *P.O. Box 266, Welland S.A. 5007.*

ASTROLOGICAL MONTHLY REVIEW. *P.O. Box 426 Leichart, N.S.W. 2040* have kindly agreed to act as a clearing house, not only for astrological queries re contacts but also for all foretelling alternatives. Please send an SAE.

A HANDBOOK OF ASTROLOGY FOR AUSTRALIA AND N.Z. This is a guide written by Jane Bennett and Craig McIntosh, published by *Greenhouse Publications Pty Ltd., 385 Bridge Rd, Richmond, Victoria.*

New Zealand

ASTROLOGICAL SOCIETY OF NEW ZEALAND. *P.O. Box 39314, Auckland.*

India

BOMBAY ASTROLOGICAL SOCIETY. This organisation was founded in 1892 and enquiries should be addressed to *The Hon. Secretary, c/o Gujarati TYPE Foundary, 196-B, Gaiwadi, Girgaon, Bombay – 400 004.*

Computer Astrology – For Calculation and Delineation

Computers have been a mixed blessing to astrology – largely good. On the plus side they have reduced the hours spent calculating charts into minutes, even seconds, thus freeing time for the actual work of astrology, the delineation, comparison, and research. (There is no mystique in calculation, just hard work and it can be done by anyone who understands the mathematics required.)

However, on the not-so-plus side, this advance has led to a rash of computerised interpretations (often known as computer horoscopes) coming on to the market which not only calculated horoscopes at prices the general public could afford, but also offered a delineation of what the calculations might mean. Obviously this was only as good as the person who wrote the data base from which all the delineations were drawn, and if they were offering a product for a keen price, these were usually very poor. Computer delineations cannot link and qualify facts as the human brain can, and thus contradictory traits often appear side by side in such readings! This aspect is discussed more fully in Chapter 9 but there is nonetheless so much to be gained in having access to a good calculation programme and a good delineation programme as an introduction to astrology that some addresses have been included here. Remember that calculation services will simply provide you with your natal chart, that is, your map of the heavens at the time of your birth, and should be quite inexpensive as they offer no analysis of the data.

Computerised horoscope readings or delineations (which provide a written analysis of what is seen) are more expensive but still a good deal cheaper than visiting an astrologer, for obvious reasons. However, care must be taken in their selection, the data base must be written by a reliable (named) astrologer whose work (and integrity) you admire, or come from a recommended organisation providing such services. Some of these advertise in specialist astrology magazines or leading nationals. Enquire with caution.

U.K.

ELECTRIC EPHEMERIS. The chief activity is selling software to astrologers, but some calculation services are available or a referral will be given. *703 Finchley Rd, London NW2 2JN.*

ASTROCALC. Also software agents, these people specialise in a wide range of programmes for micro-computers, which is what many beginners start with. There is a computerised horoscope service, also a programme called Astrotutor for beginners. *67 Peascroft Rd, Hemel Hempstead, Herts HP3 8ER.*

WHITE LEAF ASTRO-COMPUTING They will send calculations for all sorts of astrological work. Good for beginners who do not want to buy software as yet but want to learn with their own charts. *8 Maypole Close, Bewdley, Worcestershire.*

ASTROLOGICAL COMPUTER SERVICES. They will calculate for the

individual needs of the astrologer. *"Charon", 10 Myrtle Road, Ipswich, IP3 OAN.*

Ireland (and serving U.K.)

ASTRO-BRAIN INTERNATIONAL. *Glenview House, IRL Portsalon, Co Donegal.*

Europe

ASTROLABE (EUROPE) LTD. *24 Chemin des Dailettes, CH-1012 Lausanne, Switzerland.* Astrolabe sell one of the most comprehensive software programmes for astrological calculation (NOVA) but additionally for those who just want their personal chart calculated they offer that in a package with a variety of delineation programmes. Astrolabe have programmes in English, French, German, Spanish and Italian.

ELECTRIC EPHEMERIS also provide their services in French and Italian (see London address above) and in Denmark (for Germany as well) from *Norske Alle 15, DK-2840 Holte, Denmark*; and in Spain (refer to London for details).

U.S.A. (and Canada)

ASTRO COMPUTING SERVICES. Neil Michelson's calculation programmes were among the first available to astrologers and have always been to the highest standards. *P.O. Box 16430, San Diego, CA 92116.* He also offers interpretation programmes, written by Zip Dobyns' able daughter, Maritha Pottenger.

Australia

ASTROLABE (Europe). Programmes are also available from Australia. Contact address: *41 Argyle St, Bilgota Plateau. NSW 2107.* The *F.A.A. Journal* will also serve as information source in this country (SAE to *F.A.A. Journal, P.O. Box 371, Eastwood, SA 5063 Australia*).

They would probably be able to help with N.Z. addresses as well, if postage is covered. Or use the Australia service.

Graphology

As more and more headhunters use the services of a graphologist, both the standard and quality of the consultative work available improves. Graphology's tremendous advantage lies in the fact that almost anybody can get hold of a sample of handwriting, whereas the person, the palm, or the natal chart information may not be quite so accessible!

U.K.

There are three major organisations in the U.K. which support graphologists. Two of them offer teaching facilities and one offers lectures and meetings. All three would have lists of consultants on request with SAE.

BRITISH INSTITUTE OF GRAPHOLOGISTS. They have functions and courses and are open to overseas membership. *Fourth Floor, Bell Court House, 11 Blomfield St, London EC2M 7AY.*

LONDON ACADEMY OF GRAPHOLOGY. Founded by Mrs Renna Nezos-Iatrou, the Academy is a teaching and research organisation whose purpose it is to raise both the standards and services which graphology offers. Registered office (with SAE): *75b Quinta Drive, Barnet, Herts EN5 3DA.*

GRAPHOLOGY SOCIETY. This Society is more directed towards providing functions in which graphologists both national and international are invited to speak. SAE to *The Secretary, 33 Boningtons, Thriftwood, Hutton, Brentwood, Essex CM13 2TL.*

Europe

France

SOCIÉTÉ FRANÇAISE DE GRAPHOLOGIE. *5 rue Las Cases, 75007 Paris* (the London Academy is affiliated to this Society).
FÉDÉRATION NATIONALE DES GRAPHOLOGUES PROFESSIONELS. *2bis rue Roger Simon Barboux, 94110 Arcueil.*
SOCIÉTÉ DE GRAPHOLOGIE D'AQUITAINE. *9 Place du Parlement, 33000 Bordeaux.*

Belgium

SOCIÉTÉ BELGE DE GRAPHOLOGIE. *Avenue de Broqueville 227, 1200 Brussels.*

Germany

BERUFSVERBAND GEPRÜFTER
EUROPEAN ASSN. FOR THE PSYCHOLOGY OF WRITING. *P.O. Box 100803, D-6000 Frankfurt-am-Main.*
INTERNATIONALE GESELLSCHAFT FÜR DYNAMISCHE UND KLINISCHE SCHRIFTPSYCHOLOGIE (DKS). *D-7000 Stuttgart 70.* (The members of this group are university professors working in Essen and Frankfurt.)

Denmark

DANSK GRAFOLOGISK. SELSKAB. *Li. Elstedvej 5, 8520 Lystrup.*

Sweden

SVENSKA SKRIFTPSYKOLOGICA FORENIGEN. *Muraragatan 14 A, S-652 28 Karlstad.*

Italy

INSTITUTO GRAFOLOGICO G. MORETTI. *Piazza S. Francesco 7, 61029 Urbino (P.S.).*
INSTITUTO GRAFOLOGICO G. MORETTI. *Scale S. Francesco 8, 60100 Ancona.*
ASSOCIAZIONE ITALIANA GRAFOANALISI PER L'ETÀ EVOLUTIVA. *Via Renier 25/6, 10141 Torino.*

Spain

AGRUPACIÓN DE GRAFOANALISTAS CONSULTIVOS. *Provenza 238, 60, 2a 08008 Barcelona.*
ASSOCIEDAD ESPAÑOLA DE GRAFOLOGÍA. *Apartado 40099, 28007, Madrid.*
ASOCIACIÓN GRAFOSICOLOGICA DE ESPAÑA. *c/Pez 22, 28004 Madrid.*

U.S.A.

There is a Directory of Handwriting Analysts for this country which is compiled by M. Westergaard and should be available from 31246 Wagner, Warren, Michigan 48093.
AMERICAN SOCIETY OF PROFESSIONAL GRAPHOLOGISTS. *9109 North Branch Drive, Bethesda MD 20817.*
AMERICAN HANDWRITING ANALYSIS FOUNDATION. *P.O. Box 3785 Beverly Hills CA 90212.*
COUNCIL OF GRAPHOLOGICAL SOCIETIES (COGS). *7210 Knickerbocker Parkway, Hammond, IN 46323.*
AMERICAN ASSN. OF HANDWRITING ANALYSTS. *820 West Maple St., Hinsdale, Illinois 60521.*
ASSOCIATION OF PROFESSIONAL GRAPHOMETRISTS. *780 Market St. No315, San Francisco, CA 94102.*
INDEPENDENT TEXAS HANDWRITING ANALYSTS ASSN. *12612, Sunglow, Dallas, Texas 75234.*
INSTITUTE OF GRAPHOLOGICAL RESEARCH. *610 Lochmoor Court, Danville CA 94526.*

NATIONAL SOCIETY OF DOCUMENT EXAMINERS. *22 Morgan Place, Princeton, N.J. 08540.*
ROCKY MOUNTAIN GRAPHOLOGY ASSN. *3053 South Zenobia, Denver CO 80236.*

Canada

SASKATOON HANDWRITING ANALYSIS CLUB. *P.O. Box 1544, Saskatoon, Saskatchewan, S7K 3R3.*

Brazil

SOCIEDAD BRASILEIRA DE GRAFOLOGÍA, *São Paulo, Brazil.*

Argentina

P. J. Foglia, Avenida de Mayo 1316, 1085 Buenos Aires, Argentina.

Israel

NAFTALI INSTITUTE FOR HANDWRITING ANALYSIS. *52 Brodezki St, Ramat Aviv.*

Australia

Try A.M.R. (see address in Astrology section).

Palmistry

U.K.

SOCIETY FOR THE STUDY OF PHYSIOLOGICAL PATTERNS (SSPP). The Society has always interested itself in all the physiological patterns – graphology, palmistry, phrenology, and also in astrology and numerology. However, it is primarily interested in palmistry and has set diploma exams in this subject, although these are not available at the moment. It does have classes in palmistry as well as organising regular meetings with speakers who talk on the wide variety of subjects under this umbrella. Writing to them about any of these subjects with SAE may produce a list of consultants. They also have international contacts. Write to *Hon Sec., 39 Larchwood House, Baywood Square, Chigwell, Essex IG7 4AY.*

BRITISH ASTROLOGICAL AND PSYCHIC SOCIETY (BAPS) – (See address under Astrology section). Also has lists of consultants who practise a variety of skills including palmistry.

Hong Kong

HONG KONG TOURIST ASSOCIATION contains within it the SOCIETY FOR THE ADVANCEMENT OF CHINESE FOLKLORE LTD. This organisation embraces a wide variety of interests including fortune-telling skills, some of which may be virtually unknown in the West. *35th Floor, Connaught Centre, Connaught Rd C. Hong Kong PO Box 2597 GPO.*

Canada

PALMISTRY INFORMATION CENTRE. *c/o 523 W. 16th Avenue, Upper Floor, Vancouver, B.C. B5Z 1S3.*

Australia

Try AMR (see address above in Astrology section).

Tarot and Card Reading

Try the SSPP or BAPS (addresses above) or look at the advertisements in your local specialist magazine.

Other Techniques

(E.g. the Runes, Sand reading) Write to one of the general societies (BAPS, SSPP) and see if they have a consultant, or buy a specialist (occult) magazine, or write to an author who has published a title on the subject. (Your bookseller will help you with this.)

ESP/PSI/Spiritual Guidance

This is an enormous field and in many ways it is both the most accessible *and* the most inaccessible source of information to the would-be enquirer. Those bits of it which are easily accessible are more often found on fairgrounds or in local markets where clairvoyants/fortune-tellers are wont to set up a stand. Quality is as sporadic as the information: nevertheless they are worth trying on the spur of the moment because the rare gem can be found. Any signs of trying to extract information from the sitter or frighten the sitter with dire predictions or general predictions which could apply to anyone in your age-group should indicate that you have *not* found a gem, and your next efforts will have to be more careful.

U.K.

Clairvoyance/Psychometry/Mediumship/ Spiritual Guidance

COLLEGE OF PSYCHIC STUDIES. Founded in 1884, the College is an educational charity whose purpose is to further and refine knowledge about psychic matters. They have a lecture and workshop programme which is open to the public; they arrange private interviews with sensitives, and also train sensitives. They have a library and are a mine of information about this field. It is sometimes advisable to try and visit them and see what is available rather than writing, however, SAE to *16 Queensberry Place, London SW7 2EB* will find them if this is impossible. The College is non-sectarian.

SPIRITUALISTS ASSOCIATION. Demonstrations of clairvoyance and mediumship are a daily event and there is access to healers. The emphasis here is on spiritual advancement through religious means: the Association is part of the spiritualist movement. *33 Belgrave Square, London SW1.*

PSYCHIC NEWS. This is a newspaper, not a group, but they have been reporting on all things psychic for so many years that their knowledge of the field and those working in it is prodigious. Although they are not obliged to help members of the public, with SAE they would probably try to help if at all possible. Subscriptions to *Psychic News* (itself a mine of information about what is going on in this field) can be had from *20 Earlham St, London WC2H 9LW*. *PREDICTION MAGAZINE*. Again, not an organisation but a monthly publication which specialises in this entire area. Its standard is excellent and in the directory section there are advertisements for every conceivable type of psychic consultant. Weeding through them may be necessary. SAE to *Link House, Dingwall Ave., Croydon CR9 2TA*.

Word-of-mouth still remains the best source of information in this area.

LOCAL SPIRITUALIST CHURCHES throughout the U.K. (enquire at the local council chambers) will have demonstrations of clairvoyance, mediumship, and healing as part of their religious services. They often have well-known sensitives to give addresses.

Two other notable centres for healing, psychic development and spiritual matters in the U.K. are: ARTHUR FINDLAY COLLEGE. *Stansted Hall, Stansted Mountfitchet, Essex CM24 8UD* and WHITE EAGLE CENTRE. *Newlands, Liss, Hampshire.*

EDINBURGH COLLEGE OF PARAPSYCHOLOGY. The College offers information and practice on various aspects of its subject in a non-religious context. *2 Melville St, Edinburgh EH3 7NS*.

Europe

Switzerland

SCHWEIZER PARAPSYCHOLOGISCHE GESELLSCHAFT. *Zollinkerstr. 269, 8008 Zurich*. SAE to *Mrs Nene von Muralt, Weinhaldenstr. 8, 8700 Kusnacht/Zch*.

PSI ZENTRUM BASEL. SAE to *Ates AG, Guterstr. 144 CH 4053 Basel*. This organisation holds a congress every year: one year in German, the next in English.

Germany

ESOTERA. This is a monthly magazine with very good contacts in the PSI field. SAE to *The Editor, Kronenstr.2, 7800 Freiburg.*

Scandinavia

NORSK FORENING/PSYKISK STUDIUM OG INFORMASJON (Society for Psychic Study and Information). Write to *P.I.S., Postbox 5364, Majorstua, N-0304 Oslo 3, Norway.*

In Sweden most of this type of interest comes under the aegis of the Spiritualists. Contact: *The President,* FORBUNDET TRO OCH VETANDE, at *Ellingegatan 2, 21773 Malmo, Sweden.*

COSMOS. Norrebrogade 66C, 2200 Copenhagen, Denmark. This is a well-thought-of organisation with interests in the psychic field.

ALTERNATIV-NOGLEN (New Aspect). This is a magazine which publishes information about where to find contacts in this field. Buy the magazine or write to *Norrebrogade 111A, Dk 2200 Copenhagen, Denmark.*

U.S.A.

One of the great centres for interests of this kind is the State of Colorado. Joining the SOCIETY OF PSI RESEARCH AND EDUCATION may assist you in gaining access to the latest information in respect to this field. Mail to *SPRE, 1304 South College Ave., Fort Collins, CO 80524.*

A.R.E. (Association for Research and Enlightenment). This organisation was founded on the work of Edgar Cayce. It is very reputable and often organises study groups throughout the U.S.A. They are based at *Virginia Beach, Virginia.*

BROUGH JOY INC. This organisation arranges excellent conferences about subjects associated with ESP matters. Write to them at *Feather Mountain Conference Center, P.O. Box 730, Paulden, AZ 86334-0730.*

Canada

VANCOUVER PSYCHIC SOCIETY. They offer lectures, workshops, healing, reading by appointment and classes. *1887 West 2nd Ave., Vancouver B.C. V6J 1J1.*

COMMON GROUND. Not a society but a free magazine which specialises in addresses and descriptions of all aspects of the PSI and health fields, Canada-wide and abroad. *Box 34090 Station D, Vancouver, B.C. V6J 4M1.*

SPIRITUALIST SCIENCE FELLOWSHIP (S.S.F.). This is an inter-faith group who arrange many interesting workshops on spiritual development, and understudying the psyche, channelling, yoga, dreams, etc. The headquarters are in Montreal, but they have forty chapters and affiliates throughout Canada and the U.S.A. Write to *S.S.F. – I.I.I.H.S., P.O. Box 1445, Station H, Montreal, Quebec H3G 2N3.*

Australia

Try AMR (see address in Astrology section).

THEOSOPHICAL SOCIETY. Founded by Madame Helena Blavatsky (and two others) in New York in 1875, this organisation is now world-wide and encourages the study of comparative religion, philosophy and science. It also investigates unexplained laws of nature and the powers latent in man. It is well represented in Australia where it is sometimes difficult to find networks of interest in subjects akin to matters covered in this book. For information about local groups write to them *c/o General Secretary, 4th Floor, 121 Walker St, North Sydney 2060.*

Counselling

Because readings and consultations of this kind raise material which would otherwise remain forgotten or dormant, they can have a deep effect on the seeker of the knowledge, either in balancing them towards living in the future, or towards living in another world, such as the world which has provided them with the information.

Sometimes counselling is useful in reorientating the seeker and in helping with the digestion of the new information into the life-structure. For this reason several counselling bodies have been suggested. Those outside the U.K. will probably find that many of the people they consult in their own country are either linked to or have access to information about counselling bodies in their own area. Alternatively, whatever serves as a town council or local government authority usually has addresses of this kind.

BRITISH ASSOCIATION FOR COUNSELLING. They publish a directory of counselling agencies and organisations. *37a Sheep St, Rugby, Warwickshire CV21 3BX.*

WESTMINSTER PASTORAL FOUNDATION. This well-known organisation has a national network of trained counsellors. *23 Kensington Square, London W8 5HN.*

PSYCHOSYNTHESIS AND EDUCATION. Another well-known organisation with a network of counsellors. *188 Old St, London EC1V 9BP.*

CENTRE OF TRANSPERSONAL PSYCHOLOGY. The Centre has always had a very close link with therapists apart from psychologists and has a list of graduates who possess many other skills. *7 Pembridge Place, London W2 4XB.*

WREKIN TRUST. The Trust is not a counselling organisation but it is an organisation which has a tremendous programme of workshops and seminars, some of which are astrological in nature, some psychological, some spiritual, but all of which are basically directed to New Age concepts. Since the New Age is where we are all going, like it or not, it is as well to know what path we may be called upon to tread. For details of programmes, SAE to *Wrekin Trust, Runnings Park, Croft Bank, West Malvern, Worcs. WR14 4BP.*

NDE Societies and Organisations

U.K.

INTERNATIONAL ASSOCIATION FOR NEAR-DEATH STUDIES (TJANDS). *Old School House, Hampnett, Northleach, Glos. GL54 3NN.* Please send SAE.

France

IANDS. (Association Internationale pour l'Etude des Etats Proches de la Mort.) *17 rue Froment, 75011 Paris.*

Belgium

IANDS. *Rue Xavier de Bue, 30a Boite 7, 1180 Bruxelles.*

Netherlands

IANDS. *c/o Postbus 79, 1230 Loosdrecht.*

U.S.A.

INTERNATIONAL ASSN FOR NEAR-DEATH STUDIES (IANDS). Write to *Friends of IANDS, Dept. of Psychiatry, University of Connecticut Health Center, Farmington, CT 06032.* This Society sponsors NDE support groups across America.
ASSOCIATION FOR PAST LIFE RESEARCH AND THERAPY. This organisation has therapists and also a communication network for the exchange of information and experience. *P.O. Box 20151, Riverside, CA. 92516.*

Dowsing/Divining/Radionics

U.K.

BRITISH SOCIETY OF DOWSERS. Sec: *Sycamore Cottage, Tamley Lane, Hastingleigh, Ashford, Kent TN25 5HW.*
RADIONIC ASSOCIATION. *Baerlein House, Goose Green, Deddington, Oxford OX5 4SZ.* (This Association is entirely concerned with medical dowsing; it has world-wide links and a world-wide membership, so referrals, guides to training, lists of practitioners, etc can be supplied *provided* return postage is included.
RESEARCH INTO LOST KNOWLEDGE ORGANISATION (RILKO). *36 College Court, Hammersmith, London W.6.* RILKO is an academic

research organisation which carries out impartial studies on areas of information which do not seem to fit into other categories in this field.

METAPHYSICAL RESEARCH GROUP. *Archer's Court, Stonestile Lane, Hastings, Sussex.* They manufacture and retail a wide range of dowsing equipment and publish reprints of rare books on the subject.

Austria

VERBAND FÜR RADIASTHESIE *A-1070, Neutifergasse 5/5, Wien.*

Germany

VERBAND FÜR RUTEN – UND PENDELKUNDE *e.v. Kirchbachweg, 8000 München 71.*

POSTSCRIPT

The meaning of life is to see. Hiu Neng, 7th century Chinese Zen sage

Looking back in history, it can be seen that great advances in understanding occur not in a smooth manner, but in a sporadic one: long periods exist in which there is little or no enlightenment, that are then punctuated by sharp bursts in which our vision of life suddenly takes on a clearer definition.

Such a period in the growth of understanding appears to be occurring now, when tangible knowledge is reaching out to the intangible and providing a bridge of explanation for its existence.

Such a bridge is being constructed in respect to many of the so-called paranormal effects hitherto inexplicable in scientific terms. Explanations for the phenomena of healing, telepathy and all manifestations of ESP are literally around the next corner, as indeed they are – and have been gathering momentum for some time – for astrology.

The milestones in this pathway of progress came largely after the formulation of quantum physics theory which in its most broad interpretative terms demonstrates that all matter is inseparable and therefore is interlinked and interdependent. (Another way of putting it is to state that the observer *does* affect the observed – something scientists avowed never happened for centuries.) So a purely objective experiment does not really exist:* the experimenter can and does get into the act. (Which may explain why experiments with

---

* Just because it is known that the observer in an experiment does affect the result (especially in the case of PSI experiments where the energies being researched are extremely subtle and therefore easily influenced) we are not let off the hook of trying to be as objective as possible when testing ESP and other phenomena. The major criterion now would seem to be repeatability of an effect, or what scientists call replication of results.

telepathy or clairvoyance have traditionally given such inconsistent results: results which have now been categorically tied to the believing or disbelieving attitudes of those who are conducting them).*

Another condition of quantum theory defines that all matter is derived from energy, and as such energy can be conceived of as a kind of thought-form or field which brings matter into existence in much the same way as a creative idea or plan has to exist before the creative work itself comes into being, for example an architect's plan which pre-forms the structure of a house, or an idea for a book which pre-forms the writing of it. Since subtle energy fields of this nature have no technical boundaries, this may link us, on a very fundamental (thought/mind/ESP) level, not only with each other but with our environment as well, thus revealing our interdependence. An example of this kind of link is seen with greatest clarity in the instance of identical twins (who feel each other's pain and display telepathic links no matter how far apart), although the roots of such links in the broader, more general sense of person to person, whether related or not, may stretch back to the very origin of our species.

Here are some examples of how it works, both on the person-to-person (a) level and on the person-to-environment (b) level:

(a) *Person to person.* When scientists dropped live shrimp into boiling water, one after the other, plants in the laboratory which were wired up to sensitive detecting equipment that measured their biofields recorded blips with each shrimp dropping.† (Human equivalent: when an unknown person has an accident in the street, everyone in the vicinity is affected.)

(b) *Person to environment.* When researcher Frank Brown (of oyster fame – see account in astrological section) flew oysters 1,000

---

* The effects on PSI experiments of what is now known in scientific quarters as sheep (believers or open-minded experimenters) and goats (disbelievers) is well-documented. It is referred to in the works of two well-known modern researchers in the subtle energy field: by Dr Robert O. Becker in *The Body Electric*. Quill, William Morrow, New York 1985, and by Dr Julian Kenyon in *21st Century Medicine*. Thorsons, Wellingborough 1986.

† Read *The Secret Power of Plants* or *The Secret Life of Plants*.

km. inland from their sea-shore home, he observed that before they adjusted their shell-opening time to the new site there was a time-lag of some days. (Human equivalent: jet-lag.)

(a) and (b) *combined.* When American scientists* measured the emanations coming from the hands of healers (something they had been unable to do until equipment delicate enough to record the body's extremely subtle electromagnetic energy field (aura? ch'i?) was invented less than two decades ago) they discovered that during healing not only were the highly-significant brainwave patterns of the healer transferred to the recipient, but that additionally both became synchronised with the earth's electromagnetic field, pulsing at 7.83 hertz per second. This was true of genuine healers wherever they worked and however they practised their skill.

(b) In America, Dr Robert O. Becker checked the admission times of twenty-eight thousand patients into eight psychiatric hospitals and set these against periods of magnetic disturbances in the earth's field and found a significant correlation. These in turn were further found to be associated with decreases in cosmic ray intensity reaching the earth.

(b) Further experimenting by oyster-experimenter, Frank Brown, this time with mud snails, revealed that they were changing their direction in tune with both a solar rhythm and a lunar rhythm. This was considered an important experiment because it showed the dependence of living organisms' biocycles on the earth's magnetic field – which in their turn were being affected by the influence of the sun and the moon. This was redolent of research done at the turn of this century which showed that the earth's magnetic field did vary as the moon revolved around it. As Robert Becker writes:†
"all living things . . . share the common experience of being plugged in to the electromagnetic fields of earth, which in turn vary in response to the moon and sun." If this is the case, is it not reasonable to assume that we may also be affected by the more subtle, as yet unmeasured, emanations from the planets – a point which I made

* The pioneering work of Dr Robert Beck (not to be confused with Robert O. Becker) and of Dr John Zimmerman in America in respect of the phenomenon of healing is reported on more fully in my next book *Life Forces*.

† Read *The Body Electric* by Dr Robert O. Becker.

in the astrology section? If proven, these would indicate direct influences from the heavenly bodies to us on earth, forget about the indirect ones already measured through their effects on personality, such as is demonstrated in Gauquelin's experiments correlating planetary positions with chosen professions.

But it was the work of scientist and biochemist Rupert Sheldrake which began to shape our understanding of just how information may be received and passed by means other than the more obvious ones of telegraph, telephone, or tell-another-person!

Rupert Sheldrake, author of *A New Science of Life* and *The Presence of the Past** has suggested that we pass information through tuning in to each other's "blueprints" or energy-fields (he calls them morphogenetic fields). Just as around any magnet there is a powerful field that attracts iron filings, for example (entirely invisible but demonstrably present) there are fields around each and every entity and those fields, rather than the DNA in the cell, are what shape us and connect us, not only to each other but back down through the ages to our past and on into our future, like an invisible thread of continuity.†

This incredible theory is strangely supported by the work of modern scientists and neurosurgeons who have been unable to isolate anywhere in the brain where memory is stored. (See chapters on ESP and phrenology.) It seems to be a factor of the mind, not of the brain, that is of an intangible aspect of consciousness, not the actual brain-cells.

Sheldrake suggests that memory is inherent in all nature, for example spiders know how to spin webs even if they have been separated from other spiders at the egg stage and have never seen another spider or a web. This is the kind of memory that is passed from the past through to the present and presumably will go on into the future, with the species developing and improving as future

---

* Rupert Sheldrake *A New Science of Life*. Blond & Briggs, London 1981, and *The Presence of the Past*. Collins, London 1988.

† Is this line of information, this continuous thread, what psychics and clairvoyants are able to tap into when they "tell fortunes" – dredging incredible details from the past and dipping into events to come in the future as if the two dimensions of time co-existed?

generations learn from and improve on the past – a phenomenon which has been observed throughout nature. Sheldrake calls this morphic resonance and the process formative causation.

But there is another kind of memory-transference which is passed not from the past into the future but from individuals to other individuals (usually of one species) and it is certainly not done from direct transference but from something very akin to telepathy.

A fine example of this is given in respect of blue tits, and their habit of stealing milk from pecking open milk bottle tops. As Sheldrake points out blue tits do not normally stray more than a few miles during their lifetimes from their breeding place, yet the habit spread rapidly not only all over Britain but in Sweden, Denmark and Holland as well. Furthermore, although it died out during the war, when milk bottles virtually disappeared, the habit again lit up in 1947 or 1948, and once again rapidly spread over great distances, even though it is unlikely that any tits who knew how to do it before the war could have survived the interval. Somehow the information had been carried across boundaries of both time and space.

Earlier experiments on rats in the thirties showed that once they had learned a trick in one part of the world, it became progressively easier for rats anywhere else to discover the trick. But it was not until recent years that Sheldrake's principles were tested on television to see whether it was easier to solve a problem after some millions of viewers had already discovered its answer. The results supported Sheldrake to a statistically significant degree.

Research on those capable of telepathy and of psychokinesis (moving energy with the mind e.g. healing and absent healing) have shown that when they are in the mode to receive or transmit in this way, a very ancient part of the brain is activated, not the areas normally associated with our present mental activities. In most of us this part of brain activity is not accessible to waking consciousness, but in earlier times its information may have been more readily available since the homing instinct, the divining (water-finding) instinct, the intuitive instinct (needed to sense danger) are stimulated from this area.* Possibly these are skills we have suppressed as compasses, for example, and other technological substitutions for instincts and intuitions were invented.

Atavistic peoples such as the Kalahari bushmen and the Australian aboriginals still possess these skills and it is known that both can display feats of telepathy and of other forms of ESP, such as "knowing" if a relative has been hurt or has given birth, for example. They also "know" the whereabouts of friends (and enemies) long distances away and what state of mind they're in. One cannot help thinking of the blue tits and wondering whether there is not a similar link-up of consciousness. In fact Sheldrake says, in *A New Science of Life*: "it might be possible to formulate an explanation of telepathy in terms of morphic resonance and of psychokinesis in terms of modification of probabilistic events within objects under the influence of motor fields."

It is the work of another scientist who contributes yet another vital piece to this jigsaw – the previously-mentioned Dr Robert O. Becker. Dr Becker is in fact a prime discoverer of how body energy conducts itself within the body and how it interacts with the energy of the earth. Both energies are in fact electromagnetic in nature, that is they are composed of electricity and magnetism and it is a well-established scientific fact that anything that is electromagnetic has a surrounding field, from the most powerful examples, such as the fields around power lines, to the most subtle, such as the extremely low frequency fields (ELF fields) around human beings. Some scientists, for example America's Harold Saxton Burr (working from Yale) have called these fields L-fields or life-fields (when they apply to living beings) and descriptions of them indicate that they are thought to possess the same organisational capacities with which Sheldrake endows his morphogenetic fields, that is they are information-carriers, like templates.

Because they vibrate in the ELF range of frequencies, Dr Becker points out that their boundaries are technically infinite (ELF waves

---

* There are thought to be more parts of the brain involved than just the brain stem area: recent research is indicating that the pineal gland (traditionally thought to be the site of the third eye) is also activated and possibly (in the case of dowsing) the adrenal glands as well (see *The Body Electric*).

can penetrate where higher-frequency waves cannot, which is why they are used by the Navy to communicate with submarines etc). Dr Becker says that "ELF transmissions have a peculiar property: because of their interaction with the ion sphere, even weak signals in this frequency range (0.1 to 100 cycles per second) can travel all the way round the world without dying out. If an innate frequency selector is operating in this band, reception should be the same anywhere on earth." To paraphrase Dr Becker, if there is a sender and a receiver, then it would not matter how far away from each other they lived – technically the message could be received. In fact Dr Becker goes on to conjecture: "telepathy may be transmission and reception via a biologically programmed channel of ELF vibrations in the ... system's electromagnetic field." In another part of the same chapter he says, "There's now some evidence that psychic intent can influence the flow of current in solid state devices, so we may be nearing the energy levels at which extrasensory factors work."

There is one other question to be answered – and many of course to be proved – and that is, if information, as Sheldrake believes, is passed on through morphic resonance from generation to generation down the ages through the medium of morphogenetic fields, which in themselves have form but not substance, and which exist just as energy or pre-energy patterns, then may they not survive death as a form of "consciousness", an "energy" which can once again become mass when the resonance is right, in the process we know of as reincarnation? May not consciousness itself be a morphogenetic field, otherwise known as an aspect of the mind? The work of Dr Raymond Moody and others with NDEs (see chapter 8) would seem to point towards something of this nature, that is that the energy of consciousness can detach from the mass of the body and exist independently of it. In fact in *A New Science of Life*, Rupert Sheldrake does describe a set of possibilities which seem extraordinarily redolent of such a notion when he writes: "The Morphic influence of a past system might become present to a subsequent similar system by passing 'beyond' space-time and then 're-entering' wherever and whenever a similar pattern of vibration appeared. Or it might be connected through other 'dimensions'. Or it might go through a space-time 'tunnel' to emerge unchanged in the presence of a subsequent similar system." Earlier, Sheldrake makes the point that "Atoms, molecules, crystals, organelles, cells, tissues, organs and organisms are all made up of parts in ceaseless oscillation, and all have their own characteristic patterns of vibration and internal rhythm." Of course Sheldrake is a scientist and couches his thought-processes in scientific terms and not in concepts such as reincarnation, but there is an extraordinary echo between this sentiment and the long-held belief of mystics that each one of us possesses a unique vibratory pattern which persists beyond the grave and which holds the essence of the entity – some might say the blueprint of its consciousness.

That the jigsaw is far from finished is not disputed: some of the pieces have not even been painted yet. The research is very recent, and much of it is still understandably the subject of rage and rebuttal by members of both the scientific and spiritual establishments unwilling to catch up with the research of their fellow scientists and spiritualists on the front line. But that is hardly surprising, for only yesterday were PSI effects viewed officially with not only suspicion but with outright condemnation.

However even as this still goes on, the pieces of the jigsaw relating to science and metascience are slowly converging to form the central picture, and it is a joy to see this happening after so long.